THE
WORLD
ON A
STRING

AL GOODMAN AND JOHN POLLACK

THE WORLD ON A STRING

HOW TO BECOME

A FREELANCE

FOREIGN

CORRESPONDENT

AN OWL BOOK
HENRY HOLT
AND COMPANY
NEW YORK

Henry Holt and Company, Inc.
Publishers since 1866
115 West 18th Street
New York, New York 10011

Henry Holt® is a registered
trademark of Henry Holt and Company, Inc.

Published in Canada by Fitzhenry & Whiteside Ltd.,
195 Allstate Parkway, Markham, Ontario L3R 4T8.

Library of Congress Cataloging-in-Publication Data
Goodman, Al (Alan B.)
    The world on a string: how to become a freelance
foreign correspondent/Al Goodman and John Pollack—
1st Owl book ed.
        p.   cm.
"An Owl book."
Includes index.
        1. Journalists—Vocational guidance.   2. Foreign correspondents.
3. Employment in foreign countries.   I. Pollack, John.   II. Title.
PN4797.G64   1997   96-46478
070.4'332'023—dc21   CIP

ISBN 0-8050-4842-1

Henry Holt books are available for special promotions and
premiums. For details contact: Director, Special Markets.

First Edition—1997

Designed by Victoria Hartman

Printed in the United States of America
All first editions are printed on acid-free paper. ∞
10   9   8   7   6   5   4   3   2   1

To Genevieve, Sara, Yolanda,
and our families.

CONTENTS

ACKNOWLEDGMENTS

The authors wish to thank the following people, whose input and guidance on this project were invaluable: Dan Baum and Margaret Knox, Todd Bensman (*The Dallas Morning News*), Edward Cody (*The Washington Post*), Susan Crow and Peter Street, Colin Day (University of Michigan Press), Bob Duncan (NPR), Mari Paz Ferrer Calvo, Elizabeth Gibbens (*The New York Times*), Peter Grose, Rob Golden (CNN), Jim Handman (CBC Radio), Richard Harris (ABC's *Nightline*), Seymour Hersh, Stephen Hess (Brookings Institution), Andrew Isaacs, Ben Jones (EFE-Spain), Clayton Jones (*The Christian Science Monitor*), Ralph Kliesch (Ohio University), Steve LeVine (*The New York Times*), Stacy Lieberman (Wayne State University Press), Susan Linnee (AP), Bill Lyon, John McNelly (University of Wisconsin), Terin Miller (AP–Dow Jones), William Montalbano (*Los Angeles Times*), Bob Murphy, Nancy Packer (Stanford University), Henry and Lana Pollack, Amy Randall (National Writers Union), Bruce Reznick (NBC News), Everett and Stefanie Rosemond, Lawrence Sheets (Reuters), Carlta Vitzthum and Paulo Prada (*The Wall Street Journal*), Paul Tash, Natalie Watson, and Jack Payton (*St. Petersburg Times*), Marta Williams (ABC News), and Robert Wozniak.

•   •   •

The authors also wish to thank editors David Sobel and Jonathan Landreth and the Henry Holt staff, as well as the many journalists and others who are cited in the book and graciously shared their experiences with us.

free lance *n* [*free+lance*] **1 a :** a knight or roving soldier available for hire by a state or commander. **b :** one who acts on his own responsibility without regard to party lines or deference to authority **2 :** one who pursues a profession or occupation usu. in the arts under no long-term contractual commitments to any one employer or company . . . *esp* : a writer who writes stories or articles for the open market with long-term commitments to no one publisher or periodical

—*Webster's Third New International Dictionary,* Unabridged

FOREWORD

It was 1972. The Vietnam War was beginning to wind down. But tensions in the Middle East were winding up. International news organizations there were beefing up their staffs, and that was good news for me.

I had just completed a masters degree at the Johns Hopkins University School of Advanced International Studies in Washington, D.C., and was spending some time in Israel considering various career paths when I heard about an opening for a stringer at the Reuters News Agency bureau in Tel Aviv. Though I had no real journalistic experience, I got the job. I was low man on the totem pole but it didn't matter. Here I was—a young man from Buffalo, New York—working as a foreign correspondent. Once I got the bug I was hooked for life.

It was the start of a wonderful career—a career that has enabled me to have a front-row seat to history: from terrorism and wars in the Middle East, to peace treaty signing ceremonies at the White House; from an unsuccessful coup in Moscow to the Oklahoma City bombing; from the 1991 Gulf War to the Clinton White House. In short, it's been a fascinating ride. And the daily surge of excitement is still very much there.

I was very lucky. It was relatively easy for me to get that first job in journalism. At the time, many of my friends were not so lucky, and wound up in other careers. There were journalistic opportunities out there but my friends were not aware of them.

Serious journalism is very hard work and extremely competitive and is certainly not made for everyone, but for those who catch the bug, it's lots of fun. Imagine: getting paid to have fun. There are many more opportunities in print and broadcast journalism out there today even for people with no real experience—as this extremely useful book makes very clear. I wish it had been around when I was struggling to get my first assignments. The tips would have come in handy—especially the practical advice on negotiating fees and establishing contacts.

In short, if your dream is to become a foreign correspondent, you would be wise to begin that struggle by reading this book. And if you already are stringing somewhere in the world, you, too, will want to read it—it will cure you of bad habits and help you hone your skills as a professional in one of the fastest growing segments of journalism: the world of the freelance writer. Al Goodman and John Pollack, thanks to their own real-life experiences, will save you a lot of aggravation. In fact, because it can be such a dangerous world out there, they may even save your life.

Wolf Blitzer
CNN Senior White House Correspondent
Washington, D.C.
January 23, 1997

INTRODUCTION

"We want you to do an election report on camera," said the CNN producer in Atlanta, his voice crackling through aging Spanish phone lines.

"I've never been on camera as a correspondent," cautioned Al Goodman, a freelance reporter in Madrid.

"Give it a try," the producer said. "If we like you, we'll use it."

They did, and that's how Goodman got started as a TV correspondent, covering Spain's national elections for CNN.

Mere good luck? Hardly. Goodman had hustled for the chance, and stories like his are becoming more and more common. The world of foreign news coverage is in a period of remarkable transition, and enterprising freelancers around the globe are taking advantage of it.

This book explains how to become a successful foreign correspondent without first climbing the professional ladder at home. Based on the experiences of correspondents around the globe, it is a practical guide offering advice and direction to working journalists and recent college graduates who would like to work abroad but wonder how to make it a successful venture. Even for editors, reporters, or others whose career plans lie closer to Main Street than Moscow, this book provides a valuable inside look at the changing mechanics of foreign news coverage.

Conventional wisdom says that it takes years to become a foreign correspondent, that reporters must pay serious dues before landing choice assignments in exotic and romantic locales. Indeed, most staff foreign correspondents did work long and hard to get overseas, and they are among the best in the profession.

But because the number of media with established foreign bureaus is quite limited—and because competition within these organizations is fierce—many journalists who dream of landing an overseas posting never get one, even if they are capable and motivated. A lot of reporters who might well do an excellent job overseas never get the chance to prove their abilities, simply because the traditional channels of advancement are too narrow.

But there is another way to launch a career as a foreign correspondent: freelancing.

THE CHANGING BUSINESS OF NEWS

Two trends make this possible. First, the information age has transformed the media's coverage of foreign news as well as the way people view the world. Satellite coverage and on-line services bring foreign crises and international business developments directly into homes and offices, dissolving the boundaries of time and space that once kept people and events months and worlds apart. This burgeoning technology and the immediacy it has spawned are creating an unprecedented market for global news.

Cable News Network, once a solo pioneer in 24-hour news coverage, has attracted a bevy of competitors. The British Broadcasting Corporation, long the standard-setter for international radio news, has moved vigorously into global TV, as have Reuters, The Associated Press, NBC and Microsoft, Dow Jones & Co., Inc., media magnate Rupert Murdoch, and other telecom barons around the world who provide customized satellite TV in local languages. This TV frenzy and the explosive growth of the Internet strongly suggest that the news business has never before had such potential.

The long-term winners of the television revolution have not been the TV manufacturers, according to Microsoft chairman Bill Gates, but rather the companies that provide news and entertainment programming. He and others in the industry envision even more communications growth as the Internet continues to diversify and integrate the world of information.

"One of the exciting things about the Internet is that anyone with a PC and a modem can publish whatever content he or she can create," Gates wrote in a 1996 column. "In time, the breadth of information on the Internet will be enormous. Although the gold-rush atmosphere today is confined primarily to the United States, I expect it to sweep the world as communications costs come down and a critical mass of localized content becomes available in different countries."

But while the demand for news is booming, so are the costs of providing it. Unprecedented competition among news providers and the need to protect profit margins are forcing increasingly cost-conscious media to search for savings in any way they can. In the print world, newspaper readership is dropping at the very time when the cost of newsprint is rising. Staffing an overseas news bureau with full-time correspondents from the home office is increasingly expensive. It can cost upward of $150,000 annually for a full-time correspondent when salary, housing, health care, and education allowances are included. Many newspapers and magazines are no longer willing to bear the expense.

Major electronic media are feeling the pinch, too: broadcasters sometimes face satellite transmission charges of $100 per minute, while equipping and staffing a modest overseas TV news bureau alone can cost $1 million per year. These sobering economics are taking their toll, and most major media no longer maintain a comprehensive network of foreign bureaus.

"Large news organizations are becoming so cost-conscious, there's so much nickel-and-diming being done, that they're pulling out from abroad. We saw it a decade ago with the networks, then the newsmagazines," lamented Alan Riding, a veteran foreign correspondent for *The New York Times*. "A full-time correspondent costs a load of money."

Riding's perception is widely shared throughout the business. "The three main broadcast networks (ABC, NBC, CBS) virtually have opted out of regular, non-crisis coverage of international affairs, drastically reducing their corps of full-time foreign correspondents and cameramen," reported Columbia University's *Media Studies Journal* in a 1993 issue entitled *Global News After the Cold War*.

"Contractions in both print and broadcast have meant fewer opportunities," the report said. "Hiring and salaries are flat or down. Career mobility is limited. And foreign reporting suffers from a triple whammy. There is less of it, done by fewer people who must skip from place to place and story to story, often under dangerous conditions."

STAFF CUTBACKS EQUAL FREELANCE OPPORTUNITY

Now more than ever before, news organizations are actively seeking cheaper solutions to maintain their foreign coverage. And they're turning to freelancers. These independent reporters—stringers, in newsroom parlance—play an overlooked but increasingly important role in the flow of news from abroad. Just as other industries are outsourcing work to independent contractors, so are the media, particularly for work overseas where a declining dollar has driven up costs dramatically.

"Every major network, newspaper, magazine, and wire service uses stringers, especially for reports from abroad," reported the *Columbia Journalism Review*. "On a cost-benefit basis, freelancers are news organizations' most productive journalists. In a recession, when both advertising revenues and operating budgets are low, stringers are in particularly great demand."

Before 1970, only 13 percent of the foreign correspondents regularly filing stories to American media were freelancers. By the early 1990s, the freelancers had increased to 30 percent, reported Stephen Hess, a senior fellow at the Brookings Institution, in his 1996 book *International News & Foreign Correspondents*. Ongoing research at Ohio University's E. W. Scripps School of Journalism suggests that there are more than 2,000 freelance correspondents worldwide, and that the number is growing.

"Freelancers? We can't live without them," said Joyce Davis, National Public Radio's deputy senior foreign editor. "We're trying to compete with limited resources."

Even *The New York Times*, whose extensive foreign coverage sets the standard for American newspapers, is turning more to freelancers in order to save money, said Riding, who was a stringer for the paper in Mexico before being hired full-time in 1978. "*The New York Times* is the last to give an enormous amount of resources to foreign correspondents, but it's also a paper [whose management is] responding to a greater consciousness of the bottom line," he said.

This translates into a world of opportunity for journalists willing to strike out on their own. While other reporters may compete for years in domestic newsrooms hoping to land a rare posting abroad, savvy freelancers don't have to wait. Affordable laptop computers, speedy modems, and convenient cellular phone technology now enable stringers to transmit valuable foreign coverage at a very economical price. Who's buying their services? Not only the major, mainstream media, but also niche publications and news services offering detailed, late-breaking information on specific industries abroad to business leaders in all sectors trying to compete in the new global economy. The coincidence of these technological and economic developments spells opportunity; there has never been a better time to freelance abroad.

Yet all too often, would-be freelancers head overseas impulsively, without adequate planning or careful logistical preparation. As a consequence, a lot of novice stringers in far-flung countries make the same mistakes and experience the same frustrations, and many return home broke and disappointed.

It needn't be so difficult. In the chapters that follow, the challenges of freelancing abroad have been broken down into manageable steps. From choosing a region wisely to buying the right equipment to generating a freelance income from scratch, this book explains how to avoid common pitfalls and get off to a fast start as a foreign correspondent. At its core, it provides a practical, proven plan for able journalists impatient to turn their dreams of working abroad into reality.

THE
WORLD
ON A
STRING

1 ESCAPE FROM PLAINVILLE

Have you ever felt trapped? Stuck in a job so boring it begins to drive you crazy? Reporter John Pollack did once, covering a town called Plainville. Yes, it really was called Plainville, and aptly so.

Big news in Plainville, Connecticut, meant that the Town Council had ordered tree trimming on Main Street, the Public Works Board was raising water rates, or restless retirees were holding an afternoon dance at the senior center. But that didn't faze the *Hartford Courant*, whose strategy to capture suburban advertising revenue was largely dependent on daily zoned, customized coverage of towns such as Plainville, whatever the news. Simply put, there was money to be made from all the ad revenue that had flowed unchallenged for years into the coffers of small local papers.

Internally, the *Courant* classified suburban towns A, B, or C. While C towns received minimal attention and B towns a little more, A towns got local coverage six days a week. Plainville, with a population of 16,401, was an A town.

Woe to the reporter who failed to turn up a daily story. No matter what, there had to be a story, something—anything—datelined Plainville. Through sheer determination, the beat reporter scraped by from day to day, leaving even slimmer pickings for Pollack, who filled in on the Plainville beat one day a week.

Late one Friday between Christmas and New Year's, with darkness setting in and the empty streets of Plainville slick with ice, Pollack exhausted his short list of potential story ideas. An impatient editor downtown was holding space for Plainville, and the deadline was fast closing.

Anticipating such a problem, the beat reporter had left the phone number of a special source. "Call it only if you get really desperate," she warned. Out of options, Pollack dialed. A kind, elderly woman answered the phone. She ran a shelter for injured animals at her home. Pollack identified himself as a *Courant* reporter and got right to the point: did she have any news tips late on a Friday afternoon?

Oh yes! she exclaimed. A rainy autumn had caused area seeds to rot, depriving local birds of vital winter food. To make matters worse, weeks of sub-zero weather had frozen all ponds and streams, so the birds were going thirsty. Would the *Courant* urge people to set out birdseed and dishes of warm water for the finches and chickadees? Don't buy cheap birdseed, she warned; the birds are picky. And only use plastic containers, because the birds' feet might freeze to metal.

Pollack thanked the woman and hung up. With a little more time and some creative photography, it might make for a decent feature. But with the sun down and ten minutes to deadline, the story looked like thin gruel for a paper like the *Courant*, America's oldest continuously published newspaper.

"Sorry, no news from Plainville today," Pollack told the deputy bureau chief, who was editing copy at a nearby computer. Reluctantly, she agreed, and sent a message downtown saying there was no news from Plainville, only a report of thirsty birds from an elderly animal-lover.

"Do the story," came the editor's reply. "Plainville is an A town."

Groaning, Pollack quickly cranked out seven inches of copy

on thirsty birds. Professionally embarrassed, he wanted to re-move his byline. But if he did, the *Courant* wouldn't pay him the $50 it disbursed to its freelance correspondents for each lo-cal story. With rent coming due, Pollack swallowed his pride. The two-column headline on page B4 of the next day's paper read RESIDENTS URGED TO FEED, PUT OUT WATER FOR BIRDS.

Pollack was frustrated beyond words. He could handle cov-ering the Plainville Public Works Board. Its policy debates might be arcane, but they occasionally had environmental im-plications and were ultimately important. He covered the Girl Scouts without complaint. But a rush-job on thirsty birds, just to satisfy an arbitrary, ad-driven story quota?

Pollack wanted to be a reporter, but this was ridiculous. How was he ever going to move up the career ladder with McClips like this? What was his future in a town where nothing hap-pened? A seven-inch story on thirsty birds was the last straw.

It was time to escape from Plainville.

FIERCE COMPETITION FOR THE GOOD JOBS

While top reporters at the networks, major dailies, and leading magazines have fascinating beats that are citywide, national, or international in scope, many workaday journalists are stuck in Plainvilles of one sort or another. True, even the Plainvilles of the world have valuable lessons to teach, though the truly exciting stories may be rare. Young reporters do need to learn the basics in preparation for bigger assignments later, and the Public Works Board in Plainville can be a fine place to start.

But sooner or later the lessons of Plainville are learned, and it's time to move on. But where? And how? In today's world of domestic journalism, opportunities can be very limited.

Consider broadcasting. Some would argue that television stations in small and medium markets offer the best possibili-ties for advancement, though a hiring surge through the mid-

1990s has averaged only one new position per station, annually, according to industry figures. With fierce competition for these jobs, the number of qualified applicants nearly always outstrips the number of available positions. It's not uncommon for a station's news director to have a hundred demo tapes on hand from job-seeking reporters and anchors. Scott Libin, on the faculty at the Poynter Institute for Media Studies in St. Petersburg, Florida, says that although the job market is better than it has been in years, it's still not easy.

Jobs in radio newsrooms come up with even less frequency. According to a study reported in the media journal *Communicator*, more than 1,100 U.S. radio news operations have shut down since 1981, and existing stations are relying more and more on part-time news staff.

Opportunities at newspapers are grim, too. From 1990 to 1995, nearly a hundred daily papers closed in the United States and Canada, including such major metro dailies as *New York Newsday*, the *Pittsburgh Press*, and the *Dallas Times Herald*. Still others such as the *Los Angeles Times* and the *Philadelphia Inquirer* announced large-scale layoffs and early-retirement buyouts. A 1995 headline in the journal *Quill*, published by the Society of Professional Journalists, sums up the situation all too well: STARTING OVER: 300 JOURNALISTS RE-APPLY FOR 200 JOBS AS MILWAUKEE JOINS THE LIST OF ONE-PAPER TOWNS.

In such a tight labor market, even bright graduates of the nation's 430 journalism and mass communications programs can have a tough time getting jobs. According to annual surveys by Ohio State University's School of Journalism, less than 20 percent of 1990s journalism school graduates get jobs in newspapers, magazines, wire services, radio, TV, or cable TV. The rest find work outside of journalism, continue their schooling, or remain unemployed.

Ask Peter Weitzel, a former senior managing editor of the *Miami Herald*, who now teaches at the Poynter Institute. Today's job market for entry-level reporters is "someplace the other side of miserable," he said. Generally, newspapers add staff positions only occasionally, and then most commonly in suburban bureaus far from the bustling, big-city newsrooms of popular imagination. As a result, many reporters who get these jobs have little daily, face-to-face contact with key downtown editors, making it that much harder to build the relationships necessary for a promotion. Not that there are many promotions to offer: if and when reporters land a good beat, they usually work extremely hard to defend their turf.

It's an employer's market, and both editors and reporters know it. If a reporter quits, there's always another hopeful waiting in the wings. Consequently, many talented and ambitious journalists endure long years of toil in suburban or small-town beats that, like Plainville, just aren't very stimulating. The result? Little turnover, widespread frustration, and frequent burn-out.

"Dissatisfaction is on the increase in American newsrooms," reported *Editor & Publisher* in a 1994 article entitled "What Do You Dislike about Your Job?" *E&P* cited a "Journalist Satisfaction Study" by the Associated Press Managing Editors Association that found 44 percent surveyed "would like to be at a different paper in the next year." Nearly two-thirds of those aged 18 to 34 reported wanting to leave their jobs.

Even at the nation's best papers, it's all too easy to find discontent in the newsroom. "The suburbs suck the life out of you," said one reporter at the *Los Angeles Times.* "Sure, I'm at the *L.A. Times*, but not on a promotion track. They don't care. They just want foot soldiers."

Inevitably, some reporters with talent, luck, and perseverance do advance to interesting assignments in big cities, the nation's state capitals, and Washington. Some even get to write opinion columns, and a small number make it abroad as foreign correspondents. Hitting the beaches of strange lands, these reporters form an elite corps. They are relatively few, and justifiably proud.

The unfortunate truth of journalism in the 1990s, however, is that these exciting options, especially foreign correspondence, are out of reach for many reporters in print, radio, and TV. Real career advancement following the traditional path is a long and arduous journey. If you play the career game by conventional rules, odds are you could easily be stuck in one Plainville or another for years to come.

"There are two ways to become a foreign correspondent," advised Clayton Jones, who reported from Asia for eight years and is now international news editor at *The Christian Science Monitor*. "Either you hope to rise up in an organization and get sent abroad. Or you go and string."

Those journalists willing to head abroad on their own can and do find great opportunities. Steady work as a freelance foreign correspondent is challenging, rewarding, and available right now. With a little imagination and careful planning, an escape from Plainville could be just around the corner.

LIFE BEYOND PLAINVILLE

Stories of such escapes abound. Dan DeLuce spent three dull years toiling unappreciated at a suburban weekly in Sacramento, California, then worked for a year at the tabloid *Sacramento Union*. Desperate for more professional satisfaction, DeLuce (nephew of the retired Associated Press reporter of the same name) quit in 1990 to go freelance in Prague. Arriving two years before Prague became a trendy destination for young Americans hanging out in Eastern Europe, DeLuce became *The Washington Post*'s stringer in what was then Czechoslovakia. When the Balkan crisis broke out in 1992 he started taking the train to Croatia to file stories for various American papers. Eventually, he was hired by Reuters full time to help cover the conflict from Belgrade, and in December 1996 was promoted to Reuters bureau chief in Sarajevo.

In 1991 Lawrence Sheets was a waiter in Chicago whose only journalism experience was in high school, having gotten his start as a teenage Clark Kent on DeWitt Middle School's *Wee Panther Paper.* Today he is bureau chief for Reuters in Tbilisi, the capital of Georgia, in the former Soviet Union.

How did this happen? With a joint degree in Russian and International Relations from Michigan State University, Sheets was tired of waiting tables. Looking for a change and wait-listed at several top law schools, Sheets began to consider a career in journalism.

Put off by the thought of starting out at a suburban weekly, Sheets headed for Prague in late 1991. He thought he might teach English and try his hand at freelancing.

He never made it. On a stopover in Moscow to visit friends from college, he was caught up in the final, dramatic collapse of the Soviet Union. As political tensions mounted, Sheets sensed opportunity. When the nation appeared to reach a breaking point, he went knocking on the door of almost every American news outfit in Moscow, résumé in hand. Fluent in Russian, he had something to offer. A harried editor at NBC, which at that time was a partner with Reuters Television in a video news service called VisNews, was short-handed; several of his staff were out sick. With the world's greatest communist power crumbling to pieces, he needed help. Within 24 hours, Sheets had a job at $10 per hour—more than some Russians made in a week.

"The Soviet Union was falling apart. I started work in mid-December 1991. Gorbachev resigned on December 25. There was civil war in Georgia. I came in every single day for the next three weeks," Sheets recalled.

That first day he sat before a clunky, black, manual Cyrillic typewriter, banging out customs clearance forms for equipment coming in from London. Within a week he was out translating for a film crew, crowds screaming in frustration as the price of bread—deregulated overnight—soared out of reach. "It was complete chaos. The country was on the verge of collapse. People were screaming at me—they wouldn't let me out of the store. It was a good break-in experience."

Another success story is reporter Todd Bensman, who—after more than a hundred rejections from newspapers—scraped together enough money trimming palm trees in Phoenix to launch himself abroad in Eastern Europe. First from Prague and then from the Croatian city of Zagreb, he filed regularly on the war in Croatia and Bosnia for major U.S. and Canadian media. Today he is back in the United States, reporting for *The Dallas Morning News*.

Once spinning their wheels in their own respective Plainvilles, these journalists became successful foreign correspondents because they had the guts to take a chance. Nobody offered to send them abroad; indeed their journalism prospects in the United States were mediocre at best. Yet they had the imagination, skills, and sense of self to jump-start their careers abroad. They went for it, and they won.

"What do you have to lose?" asks Sheets, urging other ambitious journalists to give it a try abroad. "Twenty more years in Dullsville? You have to be creative in journalism. Nobody's going to throw it in your lap."

MANY STANDOUT JOURNALISTS
STARTED ABROAD AS STRINGERS

The success stories of DeLuce, Sheets, and Bensman are not isolated examples. In fact, many well-known journalists started out as stringers abroad. Brookings Institution Senior Fellow Stephen Hess, in his book, *International News & Foreign Correspondents*, cites some of the big names: Daniel Schorr, Elie Abel, Stanley Karnow, Robert Kaiser, Elizabeth Pond, Allen Pizzey, Caryle Murphy, and Sheryl WuDunn all started out abroad as freelancers. So did Alan Riding of *The New York Times*; Sylvia Poggioli, a familiar voice from abroad on National Public Radio (NPR); Cokie Roberts of ABC-TV; and Loren Jenkins, NPR's foreign editor. Jenkins freelanced from

Spain for *Newsweek* and *The Washington Post* and went on to win a Pulitzer Prize, as a *Post* staff correspondent, for his coverage of the Israeli invasion of Lebanon in 1982.

Even Winston Churchill moonlighted as a freelance foreign correspondent when he was a young man, filing stories for a London newspaper while soldiering in the Sudan in 1898. Coincidentally, this was only a few years after the word "string" first appeared in a dictionary as a journalistic term, describing proofs of text pasted on long strips of paper. At the end of each day, the typographers were paid based on the length of their "strings"—i.e., how much copy they had pasted up that day. The term "stringer," referring to journalists, didn't appear in print until January 1952, in *Time* magazine.

Moving abroad to string can be a great opportunity for personal and professional growth, but it's not for the faint of heart. Even for people with significant overseas experience, setting off to become a foreign correspondent can be a daunting prospect. But if tackled in the proper manner, starting a freelance career abroad is eminently feasible.

Aspiring foreign correspondents should answer several questions before deciding to move abroad to freelance (a worksheet of these questions appears in appendix 1: Is Freelancing Abroad Right for You?). One of the most important questions is: what are your professional goals? Dan DeLuce and Lawrence Sheets sought to escape suburbia for the excitement and challenge of reporting on dramatic, wrenching changes taking place after the Cold War. By contrast, Todd Bensman simply felt that his career—which had included earlier stints on small papers in Arizona and Alaska, and a previous abortive foray abroad— needed rescuing. "I went overseas to save my career and to advance it," he said. "I had to do something dramatic." Still other journalists head abroad for purely personal reasons, as they shadow a spouse or partner whose work takes them overseas.

Stephen Hess surveyed foreign correspondents around the globe. He found that stringers abroad tend to share several characteristics: they are usually younger than their staff colleagues, more likely to be at their first post abroad, and more proficient in the local language. The survey also found that women constitute about 42 percent of the freelance corps abroad, as opposed to only 19 percent of all staff foreign correspondents.

Anecdotal evidence suggests that most freelancers make the leap abroad while in their twenties. Still others get the urge in their thirties. But if your ultimate goal is to get a job at a prestigious media outfit, it's important to recognize that not everyone—even those who truly shine as freelance foreign correspondents—is going to make it to *The New York Times*, ABC News, CNN, or National Public Radio. Your work abroad may well set you apart from the competition; and then again it may not. There are no guarantees of professional advancement. But working overseas can give you the advantage of a new and challenging arena in which to showcase your talent, and one thing *is* guaranteed: personal growth. In terms of intellectual stimulation, working overseas as a stringer is a sure bet.

"There is nothing as energizing as being out in the street looking for stories, trying to figure out what the news is. There is nothing more exciting. It is such a wonderful way to get to know a new culture," said Elisa Tinsley, who freelanced in the former Soviet Union for ABC Radio, *Time*, *USA Today*, and the Gannett News Service. Today Tinsley is the assignment editor for *USA Today*'s International Edition, in Arlington, Virginia.

"I don't think I've done anything as interesting in my life," Tinsley added, "except having children."

CAREFUL CONSIDERATION
AND CALCULATED RISKS

The value of working abroad, of course, must be measured against the job you leave behind. Admittedly, there are many intangibles to moving overseas, as there are in any move or change. Even with the best of preparations, much will remain uncertain until you go, and even for months after you hit the ground. There is in every major move a leap of faith, especially when you set out for a totally foreign environment without the immediate support of friends and family. But to many people, mystery and uncertainty are part of the adventure's intrinsic appeal.

When trying to decide whether or not to go, consider the pluses and minuses of your current job, or job prospects. "I had an itch to get out of the States and see more of the world," said Michael Moffett, who left a Sarasota, Florida, TV station to become a freelance TV correspondent in Madrid. "It was limiting for me to be reporting on fires and lost dogs," he said. "If you aren't interested in where you're working, you aren't going to do a good job."

Almost every job has its joys and frustrations, and the challenge is determining where the balance is, and how satisfied you feel. Steve LeVine started work with The Associated Press in Charleston, West Virginia, just two days out of Columbia Journalism School. Ultimately interested in becoming a foreign correspondent, he plunged into the job with enthusiasm. It was a good one, and he was determined to make the most of the opportunity. After more than four years of hard work, however, he still hadn't landed that coveted promotion to the AP Foreign Desk.

"I didn't fit in," LeVine now says. "I'm pretty outspoken, and I like to do what I want to do, and don't necessarily think beforehand that I should check with the bosses."

Eager to show the AP his abilities as a foreign correspondent, he took vacation time and paid his own way to Japan and the Philippines to file stories on the fortieth anniversary of the end of World War II.

The AP bought a couple of his stories from Hiroshima and Tokyo, and one went out on the wire. But the hustle LeVine demonstrated in taking the trip apparently didn't register on AP editors, and the hoped-for career impact of his trip was nil.

"It didn't move this mountain," LeVine said. "It didn't have any impact, and all of my efforts to get out of that bureau to get to Foreign were frustrated."

LeVine yearned to work abroad, so he set himself a six-month deadline for promotion. He didn't last that long. When Ferdinand Marcos called snap elections in the Philippines, LeVine's girlfriend told him to put his money where his mouth was. LeVine decided to pack up and go, and within a month he was gone.

"The editors and old-timers looked at me with this 'What a mistake! This guy went nowhere here and he'll go nowhere there' look," LeVine recalls. A decade later, LeVine has become a veteran war correspondent, freelancing for *Newsweek* and *The New York Times* in the Caucasus and central Asian republics. "They treat me like a staffer," he said.

To many, LeVine's old job at the AP might not have seemed so dull. But for him, it had become a personal Plainville. So like countless others, he looked across the horizon and made a dramatic change.

Not everybody can escape from Plainville so easily. Family and other personal obligations sometimes preclude a quick exit anywhere, let alone abroad. But for most single journalists who feel stuck in a rut, change is as close as the decision to get up and go.

What about money? many ask. While it is true that the economics of freelancing abroad demand constant and careful attention, financial constraints that would seem to bar an escape from Plainville may not be insurmountable after all. Take an extreme example: Lawrence Sheets left the United States with large, outstanding student loans and thousands of dollars in credit card debts. Many people would say this was crazy. Once in Russia, though, and earning nearly $1,000 per week, he dispatched his liabilities quickly.

To be fair, of course, not everybody will hit the jackpot like Sheets. Indeed, most freelancers won't ever reach that income level on a consistent basis. But it is quite possible to launch yourself abroad on a very modest budget. Your most important assets are not dollars and cents, but your skills as a journalist, your self-confidence, and your determination to follow your dreams. In the end, you must weigh the cost of going abroad against the opportunity cost of staying in Plainville.

Moving abroad to freelance is not right for everybody, but it holds enormous potential for those willing to give it a try. In deciding whether or not to go, keep in mind three things. First, just about anything is possible with planning and perseverance. Second, no move is permanent: you can always come home. Third, you stay in Plainville by your own volition. If you want to head overseas as a foreign correspondent, you don't have to wait for someone to send you. If you do, you might wait forever.

Spanish poet Antonio Machado once wrote the following:

> *Caminante, no hay camino. Se hace camino al andar.*
> Traveler, there is no road. You make the road as you go
>   along.

2 CHOOSING A REGION WISELY

Deciding where to go is probably the most important decision you will make in becoming a freelance foreign correspondent. Choose wisely and your opportunities will multiply. Choose poorly and you will struggle to make ends meet.

Journalist Mike Phillips followed a girlfriend to Senegal, planning to freelance throughout West Africa while she worked on her Ph.D. After six lean months, he was back in the United States; there just wasn't much of a market for news from that part of the world, at least not enough for him to live on.

John Pollack left Plainville for Spain, moving to Madrid in early 1991 on a one-way plane ticket. At that time Spain got more international coverage than Senegal, but still didn't draw much attention in big media markets like the United States. Yet Spain was about to grab the international spotlight, thanks to a navigator named Columbus.

To celebrate the 500th anniversary of his historic voyage to the New World, Spain had arranged to simultaneously host the 1992 Summer Olympics in Barcelona and the World's Fair in Seville, launch a billion-dollar bullet train, and showcase Madrid as Europe's designated cultural capital.

Hoping to crash the party were murderous Basque separatists, planting car-bombs and assassinating police in their fight for an independent homeland in northern Spain. They would have a perfect opportunity to make international headlines, and worried Spanish officials knew it.

Yet despite nagging fears of terrorism, most Spaniards were in good spirits. The country was riding the crest of an economic boom, fueled by its membership in the European Union, the group of countries hoping to establish a giant free-trade zone in 1993. After a decade of aggressive foreign investment, Spain—once considered a romantic backwater—was fast becoming part of the European mainstream.

From a news perspective, Spain was approaching critical mass. Economics, sports, politics, history, and religion together represented a treasure trove of potential news. Within a year, media from around the world would seek all kinds of stories from Spain, and they would be looking for help from local stringers who already knew their way around.

AN OPEN FIELD

Given the impending news boom, the number of English-language correspondents based in Spain was surprisingly limited in 1991. The big British papers already had correspondents or stringers in Madrid, and the principal news agencies—Reuters and The Associated Press—ran industrious bureaus. But no American paper except *The Wall Street Journal* had a resident staff correspondent; even *The New York Times*'s Madrid bureau chief lived in Paris. A handful of stringers for American and Canadian media, like Al Goodman, already were hard at work, but there was plenty of room for newcomers.

Spain hadn't always been out of the limelight. During the Spanish Civil War in the late 1930s, correspondents (such as Ernest Hemingway) made big names for themselves writing about the battle against fascism and the coming conflagration in Europe. Decades later, the media's interest in Spain surged once more when dictator Francisco Franco died in 1975, then gradually waned again as Spain's parliamentary democracy took root.

But while the press largely looked the other way, Spain's democracy developed and prosperity arrived, as suburbs encircled major cities and cars began to snarl its modern highways and ancient, narrow streets. Officials eager to trumpet this "new" Spain planned 1992 as something of a national coming-out party, and the world was invited.

For a freelancer like Pollack, whose high school Spanish would need a jump start, getting to Madrid a year ahead of time was necessary to set up shop, make local contacts, and develop the necessary working relationships with distant editors on various foreign desks. This early start was vital; waiting until 1992 itself would have been too late.

Once there, Pollack methodically established himself as a foreign correspondent, writing first for *USA Today*, then for the *Los Angeles Times*, and later for the *Miami Herald* and The Associated Press. As he had expected, Spain in 1991 was a land of great opportunity.

BLIND LEAPS AND CRASH LANDINGS

Consider a third example. Todd Bensman, who would later freelance very successfully from Eastern Europe, made a snap decision in 1991 to quit his job at *The Anchorage Times*, move to the Middle East, and cover the Gulf War. "I didn't have much interest in what the local utility commission was doing with the telephone company," Bensman said. "The war came and I just wanted to go."

So the day after the United States started bombing Baghdad, Bensman gave notice at work. He cashed in his savings—$4,000 in Certificates of Deposit—bought a cheap laptop, and got a ticket to Tel Aviv. He picked Israel largely because the Iraqis were raining SCUD missiles on the country, and because it was one of the few places in the region he could fly to easily.

When he stepped off the plane, security officials immediately issued him and the other passengers, mostly Israelis, gas masks and antidote injection kits for emergency use should a SCUD hit with poison gas. "I was psyched, and probably a little bit naive about the danger," Bensman recalled. It was his first trip outside of the United States.

Bensman found a trickle of work relatively quickly, collecting man-on-the-street quotes for United Press International after each SCUD attack. Staying at a chintzy hotel north of Tel Aviv, he'd take the bus each day to the Hilton, where many of the staff correspondents were based. As the sirens wailed, the reporters would wait on the lawn, listening and watching for the falling missiles, the nearest of which hit a half-mile away. Then, according to Bensman, they would "pile out like ants from a kicked anthill, running for the cabs." The cabbies, it seemed, always knew exactly where the missiles had hit and the fastest way to get there. Bensman arrived with the rest amidst the smoke, flames, screaming, and soldiers, even snapping a photo (which he couldn't sell) of a SCUD's nose cone that had crashed into the front seat of a Chevy Nova.

The only problem was that each taxi ride cost about $30, and he was getting paid $20 for each file he phoned in to the UPI bureau chief in Jerusalem. With hotel bills, food, and phone calls, Bensman was going broke quickly. In two weeks, he had spent nearly a third of his money.

Bensman knew he needed to generate some cash flow, and fast. So between attacks, he networked with staff correspondents and worked the phones, trying to pitch stories to distant editors. It became an exercise in frustration. "I was talking with an Australian news agency editor, chatting it up, and thought I was making progress. Then, while I was on the phone, there was a missile attack. 'Hey, there's a missile attack! Do you want something?' I asked. 'No! Go take cover,' he said, and hung up."

In what was becoming a very humbling and expensive lesson, Bensman was learning that, in the grand scheme of Middle East coverage, he didn't count. For the most part, the only time his copy regularly made it into print was when it spooled off the fax machines of uninterested editors.

"The mistake was believing that just by being there I would be a marketable commodity. There was a glut. I was a nobody." In short, Bensman had chosen his region poorly. And things were only going to get worse.

THE COMPLEX CALCULUS OF CHOOSING WISELY

These anecdotes and those in the last chapter illustrate that the calculus of freelancing abroad is more complex than it appears at first glance. Just because the whole world seems interested in a hot story doesn't mean that a freelancer can cash in on it. Bensman, arriving late and with no competitive advantage over his staff colleagues or more established freelancers, got lost in the crowd. By contrast, Lawrence Sheets, fluent in Russian at a time when few Americans were, sprang into action relatively early in a big story's life cycle and rode its crest skillfully, even though he had happened upon it merely by accident.

Even if a country isn't constantly in the spotlight, it can still be fertile ground for a resourceful stringer, as Spain was for John Pollack. The international news focus is constantly shifting, and some very obscure countries can break onto the front page with little obvious warning. Canadian Jackie Northam was freelancing from Phnom Penh in 1993 for CBC radio when Western media interest in her biggest story—the Cambodian elections and their aftermath—began to wane. Deciding to move, she settled upon Nairobi, Kenya, as a new base of operations. Her CBC editor, Jim Handman, thought it was a poor choice. But soon after Northam was settled in East Africa, civil war broke out in nearby Rwanda. CBC rushed her into action and "she did a remarkable job," Handman said. Now she's on contract as a correspondent in Chicago for (Christian Science) Monitor Radio, and she still freelances for CBC and other clients.

SPOTTING NEWS BEFORE IT'S NEWS

Spotting where news is about to grab the headlines is critically important in deciding where to locate as a freelance foreign correspondent. In the early 1990s, Eastern Europe was the hot story as long-time communist states began their struggles toward democracy. Recently, the former Soviet republics have dominated the headlines. In coming years, Vietnam, China, and other Asian countries are likely to command more and more media attention as their evolving economies produce dramatic economic, political, and cultural change.

Scouting for major trends—economic, political, social, and religious—is vital when judging the news potential of a particular country or region. Equally important is an analysis of the potential markets for such news. If editors aren't paying attention to a particular area or can't be persuaded to take a look, you might as well forget about freelancing there.

"It's useful to be somewhere where something is about to happen that newspapers haven't caught on to," said *New York Times* foreign editor Bill Keller. "If you're not in a hot spot, you've got to write like a dream or you have to specialize. But it's hard to get by on good writing alone."

You should also go where there is a professional niche. If there are too many reporters drinking at the same trough, late arrivals like Bensman will usually go thirsty. Conversely, if there are very few foreign reporters in a country—as in Senegal—it's probably a good indication that there's little market for stories filed from there. The field may be wide open for a reason: it's rocky ground, professionally. This is not to say that freelancers shouldn't go where they want to, just that market conditions may make it harder to get started there.

In sum, the challenge is to find interesting news that has an international market, and with relatively few people telling the story. Mastering this formula is the key to choosing a region wisely.

The following sections should help you evaluate various possibilities. If you are seriously considering a move abroad, try taking notes as you answer the questions. After winnowing the choices, seek wise counsel from friends, colleagues, and family, though only you can make the final decision.

WHERE WOULD YOU LIKE TO GO?

This should be the first question on your list. After all, heading abroad to become a freelance foreign correspondent is your personal venture, and yours only. True, other people and factors come into play. But your interests and passions must guide your thinking.

As you list various possibilities, spell out a few reasons why each one is appealing. Are there political or economic developments that you find intriguing, such as the transition from communism to capitalism, or dictatorship to democracy? Are there cultural factors, such as language, dress, art, music, architecture, or food that appeal to you? Does a particular country's history stimulate your imagination? What about the climate: are you a warm weather person, or do you thrive amidst the hardships of winter? Do you seek to better understand your ethnic or cultural roots by choosing a country or region that your ancestors called home? Are you interested in learning a certain foreign language, or do you already speak one? Does a specific city move your heart? Why?

Thinking carefully about your preferences should help you identify which countries or regions appeal to you most, and why. The most fundamental element of choosing a region wisely is to select one in which you are truly interested. Genuine interest will spark your creativity, which in turn fuels enthusiasm and productivity, both essential to making a living as a freelance foreign correspondent.

IS THERE ENOUGH NEWS?

It doesn't do any good to move to a country you find interesting only to discover that nobody needs or wants a stringer there. When considering a destination, therefore, always try to gauge its potential for marketable news. Think of news in the broadest sense: politics, economics, business, sports, travel, culture, food, science, language, and crime. Almost everything that happens in the world is interesting to somebody, somewhere. The thousands of media in *Gale's Directory of Publications and Broadcast Media, Gale's Encyclopedia of Associations and Association Periodicals, Ulrich's International Periodicals Directory,* and several other mammoth reference books testify to this truth.

SEARCHING THE WORLD WIDE WEB

To get a sense of the news potential of your target region, conduct a thorough library search, taking particular advantage of the World Wide Web. This area of the Internet is revolutionary in its power, and gives you unprecedented access to enormous amounts of information. The immediacy and breadth of such information gives today's freelancers a great advantage over their predecessors in researching stories and potential outlets.

In searching the Web, look first for all recent news coverage—however tangential—of that particular destination. Try to think regionally, searching for information about adjoining countries. Remember, seek to identify major trends: economies in boom or bust; impending political change in countries that have economic or strategic importance to consumers in your key markets (such as the United States, Canada, Great Britain, or Australia); brewing ethnic conflicts in countries or regions with implications for Europe, the United States, and Canada (consider colonial history); major demographic shifts between Third and First World countries; environmental changes on a large scale; countries that host frequent international conferences and sporting events. For each of the potential destinations on your list, write down the types of stories you think you could file.

> ***Important Tip:*** When identifying potential news trends, try to associate them with specific potential markets. Who, in general, will be interested in stories on a particular subject? Obviously, it's hard to predict specific stories but it is not so difficult to identify general themes. What specific media, from obscure specialty publications to network TV, might buy such stories?

Limit your search to the past few years and note the datelines of the articles that you find. If the reporting is done from another country, it could suggest one of two things: dangerous or difficult conditions in the country being covered, or an opening for a stringer on the ground. Context should help you figure out which interpretation is grounded in reality.

If your investigations reveal that absolutely nothing has been filed, you should consider another destination, or at least broaden your focus to include more countries. Chances are, if there's been no news from a particular country, foreign interest in it is probably too minimal to make a living there. Virgin territory may well offer good material for the occasional story, however, so keep it in mind for occasional forays if you locate in a nearby country.

Important Tip: If you are thinking about working in a war zone, think again. Wars are dangerous for all journalists, and particularly for freelancers, who typically get less support from the home office, less respect from belligerents, and often lack resources that help buy greater safety. War zones must be evaluated according to different criteria. For a more detailed discussion of covering armed conflicts, see chapter 6: War Zone.

Lack of media interest in a region—perceived or real—should catch the attention of a sharp-eyed freelancer considering a potential base of operations. Such insight proved critical in freelancer Laura Ballman's choice of destination. While studying for a history degree at the University of Minnesota, she had done summer internships with *Newsweek* in Paris and the Voice of America radio in the Ivory Coast. After college, she was ready to go overseas again. "The logical choice for me was Africa," she said, "except most editors aren't terribly interested in what's going on in Africa." She went to the Ukraine instead, and there parlayed a year of freelancing into a staff job with CNN Headline News in Atlanta, where she's training to become a producer.

TRADE PUBLICATIONS ARE VITAL

Keep in mind that business stories of one type or another are often the bread and butter of freelance journalists abroad. There are literally hundreds of specialty newsletters and other publications that cover everything from computers to cigars to cement. Many of these have international readerships, and are looking for stringers around the globe. When estimating the news potential of a country or region, do some research on its economy. If a particular industry, crop, or business is important there, and is somehow linked or related to similar activity in your home country, it's highly likely there are publications that want stringers to cover it.

Countries that rarely get a dozen stories in major newspapers each year may be full of news for such specialty publications, said Larry Evans, chief of correspondents at the Bureau of National Affairs (BNA), Inc., a Washington, D.C., business publication group that relies almost entirely on stringers for foreign coverage. Citing Kenya as an example, Evans pointed out that its capital, Nairobi, is headquarters to the United Nations Environment Programme (UNEP), which BNA's environmental publications cover assiduously.

Again, the World Wide Web can be extremely helpful in evaluating a destination's news potential in its broadest sense. As you identify industries, crops, or other businesses in a particular country or region, type those key words into a search engine and see what comes up. Chances are, you will find related home pages, newsletters, periodicals, and other leads.

CONSIDER EXPATRIATE MARKETS

Expatriate ethnic communities in the United States, Canada, Great Britain, and Australia also represent potentially important markets. Many newspapers and a growing number of radio networks and cable-TV services cater to very specific audiences. If you are considering locating in their former homeland, it may be possible to file stories to these outlets. For example, it's no accident that the *Los Angeles Times* and the *Miami Herald* bought a lot of freelance copy from Spain in 1992. Both of these publications are market leaders in cities which are home to millions of Hispanics, and consequently they devote significant coverage to events in the Spanish-speaking world.

Consider, too, a country's or region's tourism industry. If it's highly developed, there is definitely a market for travel stories.

If it's extremely primitive, an adventure-travel audience might be interested. A warning is in order here: travel stories alone are generally insufficient to support any but the most established freelancer. The market exists, but it's competitive and hard to crack.

In judging a destination's news potential, make an educated guess as to how frequently you'll be able to sell the types of stories you plan to file. Include in your calculations the number of stories you've been able to find during your library search, and the time span in which they were filed. Also factor in upcoming news events or unfolding stories with international potential. Keep in mind that many feature stories are a one-shot deal, unless you file to complementary media such as a newspaper and a radio network that each want variations of the same story. The best stories are the ones that develop over time, because they can be sold incrementally, day by day, week by week, or month by month.

In short, seek a destination that has steady news potential on a variety of levels to a variety of media.

TALKING WITH EDITORS AND PRODUCERS

Ultimately, the best way to gauge potential media interest in a destination is by going to the source—the editors and producers you hope to work for once you're abroad. Try talking with foreign, feature, business, and travel editors at various media, including specialty publications, about the stories they're inclined to buy from overseas. Before you call, familiarize yourself with the publication or program, its audience, and their interests. Explain that you are thinking about freelancing in a particular region or country and wish to seek their perspective. What types of stories or particular topics are they looking for? How often might they buy stories? Do they already have a stringer in the destination you are proposing?

TESTING THE WATERS

You may decide that a short foray abroad is the best way to explore a region's potential, in addition to testing yourself as a foreign correspondent. While rarely cost-effective in the short run, it can give you a feeling for working overseas without making a big commitment. As a novice freelancer, Margaret Knox once took a short trip to Jamaica. The main lesson she learned was "that I didn't know what I was doing. Selling yourself as a correspondent is a lot trickier than writing."

In another instance, after she had gained more reporting experience, Knox flew to Koror, the capital of the Paulau Islands, a U.S. Trust Territory in the South Pacific that was holding a referendum on whether to allow American nuclear submarines to dock. A big fish in a small lagoon, Knox had access to members of parliament and other key leaders. Having previously established contact with the *Los Angeles Times*, she filed a column for the Op-Ed page that made waves in the U.S. diplomatic community because it did not promote their official position—the granting of docking rights—which was voted down in the referendum. Yet the trip was not without its professional disappointments: *The Christian Science Monitor* rejected a news piece she wrote. "I wanted to get a taste of working as a foreign correspondent," she said. "I had read of the conflict, and knew it wasn't being covered. I did it for the opportunity."

Terin Miller tried out foreign correspondence while majoring in journalism at the University of Wisconsin. Spending his senior year in India—where as a boy he had lived with his anthropologist parents—Miller needed a class project and decided to interview American foreign correspondents about "the new world information order."

Miller's only problem was that he was living in the city of Benares, an eighteen-hour train ride from the capital of New Delhi, where the correspondents were based. Determined to conduct the interviews, he set aside two weeks and made the long trip. Within days of his arrival, the short-staffed AP bureau chief Gene Kramer hired him as a stringer to help cover the trial of a major international jewel thief, at a courtroom in—where else—Benares. What luck!

Boarding the train once again, Miller—fluent in Hindi—returned to Benares to follow the trial, and filed reports day after day. He even got an exclusive interview with the thief, later convicted of murder, and wrote a bylined AP story that ran worldwide. "The whole thing was an accident," said Miller, now bureau chief at the AP–Dow Jones financial wire in Madrid.

Business writer Daniel Pruzin was already a successful freelancer in Paris when he decided to move to Southeast Asia. He knew the region well as a result of several previous visits there, but now he had to choose a specific city as his new home. So he took another trip, which helped him make the right choice.

"When I first decided to move out here," Pruzin recalled, "I scouted out both Bangkok and Singapore as possible bases." At first glance, corporate Singapore looked like an ideal city for a freelance business writer, but its drawbacks quickly became apparent. In addition to a higher cost of living, Singapore seemed to offer less journalistic freedom.

"Thailand's press is much more liberal than Singapore's, which has a tendency to suppress bad news both at home and from its neighbors," Pruzin said. "Singapore's controls on journalists and the information journalists receive are also difficult for someone from the United States to get adjusted to." He chose Bangkok.

Many freelancers make the jump abroad by seeking work at overseas English-language publications, which have flourished as English has become the dominant language of international business and diplomacy. *The Prague Post, Moscow Times, Japan Times, South China Morning Post,* and the *Buenos Aires Herald* are just a few examples of such papers, written largely by American, British, and other reporters whose native language is English.

English-language publications can give newly arrived free-lancers a vital toe-hold abroad. "You get to know the country and the players. You make your contacts. You also get clips, which show that you have written in that country," said Caitlin Randall, an American who used to write for *The Tico Times* in the Costa Rican capital of San José and now works for Reuters in London. The English-language publications are particularly useful if you don't have much journalism experience, because they may serve as training grounds not just in foreign coverage but in journalism itself. There's another advantage to such employment: meeting staff foreign correspondents, who sometimes drop by those English-language publications looking for stringers. "I was able to do fixer work for them," Randall says. She arranged appointments, transportation, and lodging, conducted research and interviews, and even did an occasional story.

Writers at these English-language dailies often moonlight as freelancers, building up their own business little by little. Al Goodman got his start in Madrid at the English-language division of Spain's government-owned news agency, EFE, freelancing on the side for eight months before making the leap to full-time stringer. Similarly, Sylvia Poggioli—now a staff correspondent for National Public Radio—was working at the English-language section of ANSA, the Italian news service, when she heard through the grapevine that NPR was looking for a stringer.

IS THE FIELD ALREADY CROWDED?

A crowded field can become a new freelancer's worst nightmare. If there are already a lot of staff and stringer foreign correspondents in a particular destination—Paris, Tokyo, and Tel Aviv, for example—you might find it impossible to establish yourself with client media or find enough work to make ends meet. Finding a professional toe-hold after you arrive is hard enough without extra competition, so don't count on getting lucky or you may be disappointed.

Stephen Hess points out in *International News & Foreign Correspondents* that American TV networks base correspondents and camera crews permanently in five key news hubs: Russia, Great Britain, Israel, Japan, and—since re-unification—Germany. The organizational design of the TV news-gathering process, Hess writes, "increasingly resembles the hub-and-spoke configuration used by most airlines."

Clearly, many print and radio staff correspondents are based in those countries, too, not just because they generate lots of news but because they offer ready access to neighboring crises. These crowded locations are staffed with talented and highly competitive foreign correspondents. Enterprising stringers may be able to find a niche in these major hubs by working for trade publications and minor media, or filling in for absent staff correspondents. But less experienced freelancers are generally better off starting elsewhere.

Given that tropical Koror was nearly devoid of correspondents and Margaret Knox was seeking only a short experience abroad, she chose wisely. Todd Bensman, with grander goals and a lot of competition, fought a losing battle in Israel during the Gulf War. Virtually shut out in Tel Aviv, Bensman realized after two weeks that he had to compete in a less crowded arena, or go home. So he headed for Jordan, with unrealistic hopes of getting an Iraqi visa there and proceeding to Baghdad. Spending a precious $80, he hired a taxi to Amman and crossed the famed Allenby Bridge. The road to the capital was dusty and crowded with soldiers, goats, and refugees. The war looked like it was getting closer. The taxi dropped him at a dingy downtown hotel—bugs crawling over the dirty carpet, wooden beds with thin mattresses, and no hot water, but only $7 per night. Its main asset? A fax machine. He was the only guest.

Not surprisingly, major media had beaten him to Amman, too. He worked the Inter-Continental Hotel for contacts, knocking on the doors of every Western journalist staying there. "I would go into people's rooms, give them my spiel and basically beg," Bensman recalled. But they had no work to offer, and he was still having a tough time selling story ideas over the phone to unfamiliar editors.

Meanwhile, the meter was running. Bensman's savings were quickly disappearing. Apart from his hotel, everything was expensive. "It was an economy set by the networks," he said. Jordanians assumed that "if you were a foreign correspondent . . . you were a bottomless pit of money." Bumming rides from Japanese TV crews and filing some copy to UPI and a few papers, Bensman held on until the war ended a few weeks later.

Crowded fields don't necessarily spell disaster. If you are a first-rate journalist and excellent salesperson, you might do well despite the competition. But you need some type of edge. As Lawrence Sheets said of his startlingly quick rise in Russia, "There was a huge door open if you spoke good Russian."

LOOK TOWARD THE HORIZON

Generally, though, it's better to look for news just over the horizon, at promising countries and regions still untrammeled by lots of resident reporters. Chuck Lustig, foreign editor at ABC-TV News, recommends that freelancers find a niche in a country "that's not being covered too well by American media."

With this advice in mind, try to ascertain how many staff and freelance foreign correspondents are already located in your target destinations, and for whom they work. Not all media work exclusively with a single stringer in a region, so try to find this out, too. Sources who can help provide this information include the foreign editors at various media and the press attachés at the U.S., British, Canadian, or Australian embassies in the capitals where you might go to live (see appendix 2: Sources and Contacts). Ask for the names, addresses, and telephone numbers of all resident staff and freelance foreign correspondents, and also for similar information about contacts in any foreign press clubs there. If complete information is unavailable, ask for a lead or two. Follow these up to solicit perspectives on the news market and confirm the number of correspondents already on the ground. Before doing this, however, be sure to read the rules of professional etiquette as described in chapter 3: Getting Ready to Go, lest you wear out your welcome even before you arrive. Contacting resident correspondents, especially freelancers, is a delicate matter because you don't want them to think you're eyeing their turf. Be sensitive; their goodwill is vital to your successful start abroad.

Margaret Knox and her husband, reporter Dan Baum, were both on staff at the *Atlanta Journal-Constitution* when they did exactly this type of research in considering a move to Africa in 1987 to freelance. They were leaning toward Nairobi or Johannesburg when a contact suggested an intriguing alternative: Harare, Zimbabwe. One person they called for more information described Harare as a "paradise," offering a great climate, direct dial phone service, safe tap water, and exciting regional news potential, as neighboring South Africa was undergoing a rocky transition from apartheid to who knew what. Best yet, there wasn't much professional competition.

"It seemed like a perfect place to go. There weren't going to be a bunch of American reporters, and there was stuff going on," said Baum, who with Knox ended up moving there and reporting on the region for two and a half years.

REGULAR TURNOVER PRESENTS CONSTANT OPPORTUNITY

Keep in mind that there is always turnover abroad, particularly among freelance foreign correspondents. In a recent survey of foreign correspondents, the Brookings Institution found that 71 percent of freelancers were at their first post abroad, compared to 43 percent of staff foreign correspondents. Significantly, the survey found that 30 percent of the stringers had been overseas for less than three years, an indication of regular turnover. Consequently, opportunities will arise sooner or later almost anywhere you go. If you choose, however, to locate in a country already crowded with journalists, recognize that you may go broke waiting for them to leave.

SPECIAL CHALLENGES FOR WOMEN JOURNALISTS

You also should consider whether you'll be comfortable with the cultural mores in your country of choice. The accepted norms in some countries may inhibit your work or pose difficulties for women, be they freelancers or staffers—even on a short visit.

Jackie Northam faced some unpleasant surprises in Saudi Arabia, which largely adheres to Islamic law, when covering the run-up to the Gulf War and the war itself in 1990–91. Working on contract as a television producer for VisNews, she was in the city of Jiddah for a story and unexpectedly found she'd have to spend the night. Her male colleagues simply checked into hotel rooms, but she had a problem: the hotel did not want to rent a room to a single woman. They considered this taboo.

She argued, but got nowhere. "Finally, a male correspondent from Finnish TV had to tell them that I wasn't going to have a bunch of men come in my room," Northam said. The hotel relented, but took precautions. "They put me in a room," she said, "and posted uniformed hotel security guards outside my door all night."

On another occasion, in the capital, Riyadh, Northam and some male journalists were enjoying the sun at a hotel swimming pool. Management singled her out and instructed her to leave the pool deck, even though she was wearing street clothes. Northam protested but finally left when management threatened to have her Saudi press credentials revoked.

She ended up buying the traditional cloak and head covering of Saudi women (for about $40), and she put it on when going to restaurants and the market.

Yet in the same region, Linda Gradstein has found that being a woman sometimes works to her advantage in covering the Arab-Israeli story. Gradstein, who's on contract for National Public Radio in Jerusalem, remembers covering the Palestinian Authority's 1994 crackdown on militant Hamas members in a Gaza refugee camp.

She was with another journalist—a male. "We talked outside to some men and then asked to speak to the women. Hamas said he couldn't, but I could," said Gradstein, who was allowed inside a private home to tape an interview with a seventeen-year-old bride whose husband had just been detained as a Hamas sympathizer.

Gradstein said that Israelis, too, sometimes patronize female reporters, offering them a little extra assistance in getting to news sites.

WHAT IS THE COST OF LIVING?

Making a living as a foreign correspondent depends not just on your ability to find stories and market them successfully, but also on the cost of operating in your destination of choice. Living and working as a correspondent in Paris is a much more expensive proposition than setting up shop in, say, Paramaribo, the capital of Surinam. Paris, rich in political and cultural news and crowded with correspondents, is one of the most expensive capital cities in the world. Paramaribo, seldom in the headlines and practically devoid of correspondents, is among the cheapest. A freelance foreign correspondent would have to sell a lot of stories to make ends meet in Paris, but relatively few in Paramaribo.

This is not an argument for setting up shop in Surinam, per se. In reality, one should look for a destination with greater news potential. But it does highlight the fact that making a living is all relative. It is absolutely essential to take living expenses into account when evaluating the feasibility of a particular destination. Therefore, try to select a destination with enough marketable news to make ends meet.

Below is a checklist of major costs associated with living and working abroad as a journalist, and some suggested sources of information that you should contact when considering options for your new home base. The purpose of this checklist is to help you develop an estimated monthly budget. Armed with such numbers, you can better judge whether or not a country's news potential is great enough to cover your operating costs.

Rent
Renting a room or apartment—which is likely to double as an office—can be a freelancer's single biggest monthly expense. Housing conditions and costs vary widely from country to country, so it is especially important to seek specific, up-to-date information on each destination you are seriously considering.

Investigate the full range of potential housing options: inexpensive hotels, single rooms in private homes, boarding houses, apartments, and rented houses. Find out the costs associated with each (including security deposits), and their availability.

Keep an open mind. You might end up paying $350 for a small room in a shared, unheated apartment that gets so cold you have to type your stories wearing woolen mittens—as John Pollack did in Madrid one winter—or you might end up in the lap of luxury. In Zimbabwe, Dan Baum and Margaret Knox lived extremely well as freelancers, buying a used car and renting a house that came with its own gardener and housekeeper. They even shared a receptionist at their downtown office, all for about $1,100 per month. "It was nice," said Baum, who now writes books and freelances from Montana, where he lives with Knox, a fiction writer.

Bangkok-based Daniel Pruzin, who specializes in business strings, confronts a higher cost of living in Asia, where housing in major cities tends to be expensive. In Bangkok, even a one-bedroom apartment in a dilapidated building can cost $500 per month, while a decent two-bedroom place with all the Western amenities costs between $2,000 and $4,000 per month, "thanks to unscrupulous property developers and large foreign corporations with generous housing allowances for their expat employees." And office space? "I work out of my home; no sense commuting in this town where it can take an hour to go two blocks," Pruzin said.

Other Asian cities, particularly Hong Kong and Singapore, are even more costly, Pruzin said. Freelancers there should be prepared for "small, one-bedroom places way up in elevatorless apartment buildings."

Depending on the country, you might get the best deal paying in American dollars, British pounds, or other hard currencies. A good place to begin your inquiries is at your target country's embassy or consulate in your own country (i.e., the Brazilian embassy in Washington, D.C., or the French embassy in Ottawa). Calling is preferable to writing because your request—hardly a high priority for the diplomatic corps—is less likely to get lost in the shuffle. When you inquire, don't mention that you are seeking work in that country, because their attention may shift to the requirements for your working papers. Tell them you are interested in studying the language in their country or taking an extended vacation, and are trying to get information about housing costs. Information officers at American, Canadian, and British embassies and consulates in your target countries also may prove helpful.

In addition, if you currently live in a community with a significant immigrant population from the country or region you are considering, seek advice from them. Most people are happy to talk about their homeland, and may have friends or relatives still there with good information or inside leads. Another good source of information are study-abroad programs run by American and British colleges and universities. They often place students with families, and therefore have information on housing costs in a number of countries. Finally, don't overlook the alumni association of your alma mater. Does it have an active chapter in your target destination, or a list of graduates living there? These people might be especially inclined to give you good advice.

Food
Try to ascertain the likelihood of getting a place with kitchen privileges. Cooking for yourself is usually the cheapest way to eat, so try to find out the cost of a market basket of groceries. Or if you are going to eat out often, you need to factor that into your budget.

Tourist guidebooks, particularly those aimed at budget travelers, typically describe the average meal prices at modest restaurants. American, British, or Canadian consular officials located in that country also may provide useful information, and the same is true of study-abroad programs at colleges and universities. And don't forget the possibility of posting queries on the Internet.

Calculate your monthly food budget based on a combination of eating at home and in cheap restaurants. You need to eat to be productive, but unless you're an excellent cook, you probably won't be eating gourmet meals until after you sell some stories.

Transportation

Depending on where you go and the types of stories you intend to file, transportation can be a significant factor in your operating costs. If you intend to cover a broad region, you will need to account for travel expenses. This usually includes both public transportation—taxis, buses, rickshaws, trains, planes, subways, or ferries—or private transportation, such as a rental or privately owned car.

If you are working in a big city, public transportation is probably adequate for most day-to-day needs. Again, budget travel guides are often a good source of information about public transportation costs around the world, as are travel agents with overseas operations, such as American Express.

In some countries you might need a four-wheel drive vehicle; in war zones with heavy fighting, an armored personnel carrier. In some situations a bicycle might be the best way to get around. Except for hitchhiking, which can be quite unpredictable, it all costs money.

When calculating your monthly transportation costs, try to determine if some of the stories you'll file involve travel. If so, where and how often? Most media are loath to incur big travel expenses with regard to stringers, especially at the outset. Also remember that even if they do agree to pay expenses you may have to front the money and wait for reimbursement. To reduce unnecessary travel expenses, plan on a) locating near the news; b) using the telephone; and c) taking advantage of public transportation whenever possible.

> ***Important Tip:*** Outside the United States, the cost of gasoline can be prohibitive. In Western Europe, it's about three times the price in the United States. Cars, even used ones, tend to cost twice as much as similar models in America. There are also the potential urban problems of parking and theft. So it's best not to plan on buying a car overseas right away. Postpone that decision until you fig-

ure out your actual transportation needs and start making steady money.

Telecommunications
Since you will be filing most stories via electronic communications—by modem, fax, or phone—you need to include these
costs in your projected budget. Although the telecommunications world is fast changing, many foreign governments still
have a monopoly on phone service, usually providing poor service at high prices. In recent years, however, British, Canadian,
and American long distance carriers have struck deals with
many countries that enable travelers and expatriates to exploit
cheaper international rates. These rate schedules are readily
available from AT&T, Sprint, MCI, British Telecom, and Bell
Canada.

Shop around. Talk with phone-service representatives, explaining that you may be moving to Zambia, or France, or Ti-
bet and that you'll need to call the United States, Canada, Great
Britain, and Australia. Ask if their company provides international long distance service from that country. How much does
it cost? Are there discounts at certain times or for frequently
called numbers? How about discounts for heavy usage? Ask
the representative to send you a price list.

To ascertain the cost of calls within a target nation, both local and long distance, consult travel guidebooks and the embassy or consulate of that country. You are unlikely to have
many choices here, but try to factor these local phone costs
into your projected budget, even if they are only crude esti-
mates.

MOBILE PHONES
Don't forget to investigate the availability of mobile phone service in your target region and the geographic limitations associated with specific equipment, which may vary drastically
from country to country. Digital mobile phones—specifically

those phones operating on a system called the Global System for Mobile Communications (G.S.M.)—are catching on rapidly outside of the United States. In 1996, G.S.M. phone coverage included forty countries in Europe, North Africa, the Middle East, Asia, and the Pacific. Unfortunately, rates for mobile phones are almost always higher than rates for traditional, ground-based communications, although the cost of mobile communication is dropping.

One disadvantage of G.S.M. phones is spotty coverage in some countries where the service is offered. You can often get better coverage within individual countries using less technologically advanced analog mobile phones, which also let you dial internationally but cease to function if carried out of that country. You should choose a G.S.M. or analog phone depending on how much traveling you'll be doing between countries. Al Goodman's main beat is Spain, so he uses an analog mobile phone that works in about 95 percent of the country (almost anywhere but way up in the mountains).

E-MAIL

While mobile phones outstrip the clumsy bureaucracies of many foreign telephone companies, the explosive growth of on-line services is quickly making e-mail the preferred communications tool of far-flung stringers and editors alike. It is fast, convenient, and fairly reliable both as a means of daily communication and filing stories. It also does away with the headaches of disparate time zones and the costly hassles of phone tag. With this in mind, contact on-line service providers at home about access abroad.

Administrators and students at foreign universities might also be able to provide valuable information about local Internet access; those institutions which are hooked into the Internet can be reached on-line, even in many countries with antiquated infrastructures.

Commercial Internet access providers are becoming more

common abroad, even in countries whose visible infrastructure might belie their presence on the information superhighway. In Kenya, where local phone rates to the United States top $5 per minute, stringer Patricia Reber pays $20 per month for basic e-mail service, which she uses to file to *USA Today* and other clients. Full Internet access, necessary to read wire service news, is available but costs much more.

Unfortunately, e-mail does not suffice for communications within Africa, Reber said. "Phoning within Kenya often means five or six tries, if you get through at all. Phoning from Kenya to other African countries is even worse—and expensive! I have easily spent $300 to $400 on one article involving calls outside Kenya," Reber said. "Without a doubt, communications—or the lack thereof—is the most frustrating thing about life here."

But while filing stories may still be inconvenient and sometimes costly, recent technological advances are a far cry from the primitive communications even a few years back. Dan Baum recalls one stifling night when the desk clerk at his Kampala, Uganda, hotel pounded urgently on his door. The international line he had scheduled to send a telex to the United States was finally ready, come quickly!

With a telex—essentially a stone-age version of e-mail—a message could be typed directly into a keyboard for transmission, or, in the case of long stories, recorded ahead of time via a pattern of holes on long strips of paper, which a person would then feed into the telex machine for transmission.

Correspondents sometimes chose hotels simply for their telex machine. This particular establishment, which Baum recalls as "The Diplomat" or "The Ambassador," beat out several others that stank of feces and buzzed with flies. Its telex was one of its few redeeming features, and Baum leapt out of bed.

Grabbing his story—a bale of yellow paper telex tape—he made a dash for the hotel lobby. Running down the hall, shirtless because he was in such a hurry, a loop snagged on a doorknob, and the tape—his story—ripped in half. Which end was which? He didn't know. Feeding the tape in, the second half went first, followed by the lead. It didn't matter: as soon as he had sent it, a terse message came across the telex printer from the *San Francisco Examiner*: "May not use story because of events in Gulf."

"What happened in Gulf?" Baum tapped out, hurriedly.

"U.S. frigate hit by Iraqi missile," came the reply. "38 dead. Must go now."

And the telex fell silent.

TOTALING UP COSTS

Combining the cost of these four components—rent, food, transportation, and telecommunications—will provide an estimate of the minimum monthly cost of living in a particular country. Then factor in your personal needs: everybody's lifestyle is different, and you should be comfortable enough to work effectively.

Building up an income as a freelance foreign correspondent could take time, so it's best to plan on zero income for at least two or three months. During this period, you will be living off of savings. Check the exchange rates over the past year, seeking to gauge how long your savings will last. Don't forget to allow for a security deposit on housing. Then add the cost of your initial outlay for equipment (see chapter 3: Getting Ready to Go), include the price of an airline ticket to get there, and you have your startup costs.

DOES IT ALL ADD UP?

Having calculated startup costs and monthly operating expenses, reconsider the country's news potential. Find out how much various media pay for stories from abroad. One source for general freelance rates is the *National Writers Union Guide to Freelance Rates and Practice*, available in bookstores or from the NWU in New York (see address in appendix 2: Sources and Contacts). It contains fees, contracts, and working conditions in every major freelance genre, including journalism. In general, metropolitan newspapers in the United States pay $150–$200 for an 800-word story. Other publications pay word rates, from 15 cents to $1 per word, the latter from so-called glossy magazines in New York and Los Angeles. Radio news spots generally pay $20–$50 each; you may get up to $100 for a TV voice-over of video, and $250 or more for producing TV news packages. Of course, these rates are only rough guidelines. Your actual pay will depend on a variety of factors.

Try to estimate, conservatively, how often you'll be able to file stories. Does it appear that you can earn enough to make ends meet? Remember, circumstances on the ground, especially news, will inevitably vary over time. This type of analysis, however, should enable you to effectively compare the feasibility of destinations as distinct as Cologne and Khartoum.

Juan Tamayo, a veteran foreign correspondent and former foreign editor of the *Miami Herald*, offers this advice: "You have to look for a story that is hot enough for people to buy, easy enough to get, and taking place in a place cheap enough so you can make ends meet."

MAKING UP YOUR MIND

In making a final decision about your destination, weigh the intangible collateral benefits each might offer. These are benefits unrelated to professional gain and are, for many people, just as important. Some people look upon a move abroad as a chance to learn a foreign language. Others seek the opportunity to simply revel in a different culture, or to gain a fresh perspective on the world or on their own lives.

In the end, you make the choice. There are no guarantees that you will succeed as a freelance foreign correspondent, even if you choose your destination wisely. But your chances of success are much greater if you choose carefully, rather than making a blind, impulsive leap.

3 GETTING READY TO GO

E ven if you're like Margaret Knox, heading for the South Seas, going abroad as a foreign correspondent is no tropical vacation. All too often, freelancers stumble after they arrive, realizing that many important preparations should have been taken care of before leaving home. Todd Bensman found that out the hard way, jetting off to the Middle East without first laying the groundwork. Aggressive planning before departure is essential if you hope to hit the ground running, and this chapter lays out exactly what needs to be done. If you do your advance work right, it will start paying off the moment you arrive.

LINING UP CLIENTS AT HOME BEFORE YOU GO

Once abroad, your income will largely depend on your working relationships with editors and producers back home, because they decide whether to buy or reject your stories. Therefore, your primary task before heading overseas is to contact at least some of your future clients and start making solid connections.

This is no easy task. Editors and producers often complain

about being overworked, and talking to freelancers is rarely their top priority. This makes it doubly important that you establish substantive contact with them before you go, because they are unlikely to rely on a distant journalist with whom they're not familiar. "I have no reason to believe they're competent," said John Simpson, editor of USA Today's International Edition. "I usually find that people who query us cold don't know the publication [and] don't know news."

It is absolutely critical to familiarize key editors and producers with your name, background, and abilities before you leave home. "See the whites of their eyes before you go," said Alan Riding of The New York Times, or at least talk with them on the telephone. "Don't land in a place and *then* think about who you're going to write for." There will be many times when you call an editor or producer collect from overseas with a story to pitch, and the last thing you want to hear is: "Who? Calling from where? No, I can't accept the charges."

MAKE A LIST OF POTENTIAL CLIENTS

The first step is determining which media might be interested in stories from your intended destination; the second is identifying which editors or producers to contact. Generally, international and foreign editors (and their foreign desk colleagues) will be your main contacts, as well as producers responsible for international news. Many of these may have worked overseas themselves, some even as freelancers. Other key editors are likely to be those from the business, travel, and feature departments.

Start by assembling a list of potential clients—print and broadcast, mainstream and specialty—for whom you might conceivably file stories. Cast your net broadly, starting with the variety of media industry publications, which are generally available at the reference desks of good libraries. Expect significant overlap among these sources. Another great resource is the World Wide Web.

SEND A PACKET, THEN FOLLOW UP

After selecting your target media and identifying the relevant editor and producers, prepare a packet that includes a résumé, clips and/or demo tapes, and a cover letter. The letter should describe who you are, where you're going, and what you intend to cover that might interest them. After sending the packets, alert editors and producers of their impending arrival with a timely call or e-mail. Follow up again after they've had a chance to review your materials.

Todd Bensman, after going broke on his impulsive, poorly planned freelance foray to the Gulf War in 1991, approached the endeavor very differently before his second stint abroad. In 1992, he identified Eastern Europe as fertile ground for a freelancer and zeroed in on Prague as a convenient and economical base of operations. Next, he gave himself six weeks to establish contacts with potential clients. This was a reasonable amount of time, but it could have been longer. He sent them clips, a résumé, and a cover letter. Then he began an all-out phone assault. He called some media two or three times to confirm that his clips were on file, to discuss what types of stories they liked, and—importantly—to get the name of the person who would accept his collect calls from Europe.

"I set everything up," Bensman said. "I made damned sure they knew my name before I left, and the stories I was going to file." Freelancers who fail to make effective contact with newsrooms before they go will face only more frustration later. "You're going to blow it if you don't set it up in advance."

Recognizing this, Dan Baum and Margaret Knox also contacted editors and producers well before departure, conducting their search for clients as if they were applying for a job, which in essence they were. "We made up a very slick packet," Baum said, including the requisite résumés, clips, and cover letter. "We sent this to every foreign editor in the country and said, 'If you're interested, give us a call.'" Baum and Knox kept a follow-up questionnaire next to the phone, so that when an editor called they could systematically explore the types of stories that interested a particular publication or program. Ultimately, six editors and producers agreed to accept collect calls from Baum and Knox in Africa, and made technical arrangements to receive the pair's copy and audio reports.

It was an encouraging response for the duo, who at this point were each experienced journalists and determined to report from abroad without first climbing the ladder in Atlanta for ten years. Knox's periodic forays abroad had been bolstered by a Master's degree in Journalism at the University of Michigan and five years of reporting at the *Atlanta Journal-Constitution*, while Baum—also a reporter at the paper—had spent a year in Singapore on staff at *The Wall Street Journal*'s Asian edition. He had landed that coveted job at the age of twenty-six through almost fanatical persistence, sending the editor a cover letter and fresh clips every week for eight consecutive months. Notably, most of these clips came from *Energy User Daily* in New York, where Baum and his colleagues worked seventy-five hours a week "viciously determined to become Woodward and Bernstein." Baum described that publication as "the lowest, bottom-feeding job in journalism." (*Energy User Daily*'s editor, Robert Olen Butler, would go on to win the 1993 Pulitzer Prize for Fiction for his book of short stories about Vietnamese immigrants, *A Good Scent from a Strange Mountain*.)

Not everyone planning to freelance overseas will have résumés of the caliber that Baum and Knox compiled before moving to Africa, but lack of journalistic experience need not inhibit your ambition. With fluent Russian but no reporting experience, Lawrence Sheets did extremely well on his first try. Confidence and common sense go a long way, and if you haven't worked much as a reporter, emphasize instead your language capabilities or relevant academic background, or whatever else suggests that you bring at least some developed skills to the job.

The packets you send to editors should include your e-mail address as well as a self-addressed, stamped postcard with the typed message containing two options:

_____ Yes, I am interested in stories from (your destination). Please keep in touch.

_____ No thanks, I am not interested.

The card should include the editor or producer's name and the medium. This system enables harried news executives to quickly check off one option and drop the card in the mail. The truly uninterested will simply toss it in the wastebasket, but even if editors or producers fail to return your postcard, you don't have to scratch them from the list. Recognize, however, that until you demonstrate your abilities abroad, you may have a hard time persuading them to buy your stories. Some newsroom executives, instead of returning the postcard, may simply zap off an e-mail response, or visit your Home Page on the Web, if you've got one. They may even refer you to colleagues in other departments or at other media.

Al Goodman used the postcard technique before coming to Spain and received about twenty replies out of 50 postcards mailed. Even some of the ones marked "no thanks" came back with handwritten encouragement, or with other suggestions, such as "Why not contact the editor at such-and-such publication?"

The *Dallas Times Herald* was one of the papers that responded positively, and Goodman filed several stories to it soon after his arrival in Madrid. (The *Times Herald* later went out of business, but thankfully not before paying Goodman for his work.)

Allow a few weeks for the editors and producers to respond, and follow up immediately with those who express interest.

Keep in mind that most will tell you how tight their budgets are, and that they use little freelance work. This may be true, but the bottom line is that good freelancers are extremely cost effective, and if you do good work you'll find a market for it.

For instance, the *Miami Herald* sometimes buys freelance copy from countries outside the realm of its primary overseas focus, Latin America, simply because a particular stringer is talented and has an excellent story idea. "You never have enough money to buy everything they offer," said Juan Tamayo, but the foreign desk tries to cultivate a professional relationship that both benefits the paper and enables the stringer to make ends meet. The important thing about these stringers, added Tamayo, is that "we know them; we know the quality of their work."

WHEN TALKING WITH POTENTIAL CLIENTS, BE BRIEF BUT THOROUGH

Like your cover letters, your exploratory conversations with editors and producers should be brief, but cover several key points: do they already have a regular or semi-regular stringer in your target country? If so, will there really be enough work for more than one, and would you be stepping on the existing stringer's turf? (See chapter 4: Stranger in a Foreign Land.) If the editor has a stringer in your destination but encourages you, too, it may indicate dissatisfaction with the existing stringer's work, or that the freelancer is overextended and unable to respond to their requests, or that the resident stringer is skilled at only certain types of stories, such as breaking news or features.

"You always have to have backup," said *USA Today*'s John Simpson. For example, in 1996, his paper relied on two stringers in Jerusalem and one in Tel Aviv. *USA Today*'s Elisa

Tinsley, who supervises these stringers, said "they don't tend to step on each others' toes too much."

"We look for stringers who are reliable with information and who can be located on short notice," said CNN producer Rob Golden. "Those same stringers must have quick and ready access to information, either by already working at another news organization or by being able to make a few phone calls to the right people."

In your initial conversations with editors, try to pitch some stories pegged to an upcoming news event (such as elections), or a feature you think you could deliver soon after your arrival overseas. If you've done your homework, you should have a decent idea of what industries or businesses or cultural topics are relevant to the clients' readers, listeners, or viewers. Remember to listen to your potential clients describe the kinds of stories *they* want.

All too often, inexperienced stringers pitch stories with marginal relevance, *USA Today*'s John Simpson said. "They offer inside baseball from goodness-knows-where when that's not what the general interest reader is going to be interested in, or at least not what a *USA Today* reader is going to be interested in." Juan Tamayo recalled one freelancer who pitched a story to the *Miami Herald* about "water lily infestations on Lake Tanganyika." Tamayo passed on the opportunity. "They just don't realize they're selling a product."

NAIL DOWN THE MECHANICS OF FILING

While you've still got the editor or producer on the phone, ask how they prefer to get story pitches: by e-mail, by fax, or by phone. If he or she expresses genuine interest in your work and target destination, inquire about the exact logistics of filing stories. These specifics can vary significantly and will also depend on the communications available in your destination. The ideal method is filing via modem directly into that news organization's central computer, using a local access number overseas. Often, media's technical support staff know more about this than harried editors, so talk to them if possible. Bits and bytes and baud rates are a lot easier to decipher before leaving home, rather than when you're struggling to make a connection, deadline closing in, from some noisy telephone booth in a distant foreign capital. If possible, try sending a short test message to the computer system before heading abroad.

Before hanging up with the editor or producer, get the names, e-mail addresses, and direct phone and fax numbers of the key editors and their assistants on the foreign or international desk. Last, inquire about pay rates, and how to submit invoices (electronically or by mail). Find out how long it takes to get paid, and in what currency. Don't be surprised if the editor or producer is too busy or unwilling to discuss the details of what is still a hypothetical relationship. Be polite, but don't be deterred: offer to speak with an assistant. For a detailed approach to this financial nitty-gritty, see chapter 5: Making Ends Meet.

> ***Important Tip:*** You have a lot of ground to cover in this phone call, so tackle it in an organized manner. Use a prioritized checklist of questions, and stay attuned to the mood of the person with whom you're speaking. If you're concise and move right along, it is more than likely that the editor or producer will be impressed by your thorough and professional approach.

IDENTIFYING PROFESSIONAL CONTACTS
ABROAD BEFORE YOU GO
. . . .

Your income abroad may not depend exclusively on clients back home. If you can identify some potential customers abroad before leaving home your arrival overseas will go much more smoothly. English-language publications and foreign bureaus of The Associated Press and other wire agencies can provide critical, early income for novice freelance foreign correspondents.

Researching his second foray abroad, Todd Bensman read about two English-language papers in Prague and called both before leaving the United States. The editor of one said she could guarantee work, and would pay in Czech crowns. That phone call led to his first clip when, shortly after arriving, he wrote a story for *The Prague Post* about a Czech peacekeeping contingent departing for duty with the United Nations in Croatia.

Steve LeVine laid similar groundwork before departing for the Philippines, letting the AP bureau chief in Manila know of his impending arrival. These types of contacts may not lead to immediate work, but they can provide starting points from which to network after landing. So before your departure, compile a list of such possibilities in your destination: wire service bureau chiefs, resident staff correspondents, freelancers, local journalists, academics, business executives, and anyone else who might be able to offer advice.

Compiling this list requires some resourcefulness, particularly when you are thousands of miles away. Start the list by contacting AP and AP–Dow Jones, Reuters, UPI, Bloomberg Business News, and other news services to determine if they have an active bureau in your destination. If so, write to the bureau chief, explaining that you are a journalist soon moving to that country, and that you hope to solicit their advice after you arrive. Don't ask for a job in this letter. Although many bureaus do hire some of their correspondents locally, few are hired sight unseen. Asking for a job right off the bat may only put a bureau chief on the defensive, although he or she will surely know that you want work even if you don't ask. Your chances of getting a job are much better if you've already proven yourself in the field. Your letter *will* alert them to your impending arrival, however, and you never know when they might have an opening.

If there isn't a wire service bureau in your destination, locate the control bureau (usually in a neighboring country) whose responsibility it is to monitor news where you'll be living. Write to that bureau chief, offering your services as a stringer and offering to contact the bureau again once you have landed in-country.

Don't get discouraged if a bureau chief is brusque about your query: most of them get lots of inquiries from would-be stringers. "I get endless calls from people who say 'the Foreign Desk said to call,' which means that the Desk is just panning them off on you," said Alan Riding of *The New York Times*. There's nothing you can do about this. Competition is competition, and bureau chiefs are always busy; just be honest, do your best, and make the contact.

If you currently live near a college or university, consider seeking out foreign students from the country you are moving to, as well as professors in relevant fields, to ask them for advice and contacts. Don't overlook university study-abroad programs, and seek advice from any expatriates who may live in your community. Multinational corporations, high-tech research companies, laboratories, and other institutions with an international outlook frequently have foreign scholars or executives in residence. If you've got a lead in one of these organizations, follow it up.

This process is in essence a fishing expedition, and you are casting about for any information that could be useful after you arrive at your destination. Serendipity plays a role here, but only if you give yourself a chance. How long should your list of contacts be? That depends on where you're going and how aggressive you are in your research. The more the better, but six to twelve leads are generally enough to get you started.

BASIC LOGISTICAL PREPARATIONS: DON'T LEAVE HOME WITHOUT THEM

Nearly as important as your professional networking before departure are the myriad logistical concerns of setting up a solo bureau overseas. Thinking them through and handling them ahead of time will save you incalculable time, money, and aggravation once you're overseas.

Passports and Visas
If you don't have a valid passport, apply for one right away. U.S. post offices provide passport applications, but processing can take up to ten weeks. Factor in that delay when choosing your departure date. When you get pictures taken for the application, err on the side of respectability in your appearance; you don't need hassles from suspicious guards at foreign borders. While you're at it, print a dozen extra photos for future visa applications, press credentials, and other forms of identification.

Next, investigate how to obtain visas and working papers as a journalist for your target country. This is a potentially delicate task, because many countries, plagued by unemployment, are suspicious of any foreigner who seeks a job. Foreign correspondents are particularly suspect, especially in nations that lack the tradition of a free press. As such, consular officials may be unsympathetic to your inquiries. So be discreet when you ask the relevant officials about visas and working papers. Inquire over the telephone, and—without seeming evasive—

don't give your name until you actually apply for a visa. This way, if you must apply for a tourist visa because that's the only practical means of getting into the country, nobody's the wiser about your intentions.

Traveling between countries may require you to apply for various visas and other permits locally—that is, once you're already abroad. At best this is inconvenient; at worst, a bureaucratic nightmare. In these cases, patience is a virtue. Working in rural Africa, Dan Baum and Margaret Knox carried a rubber stamp-making kit to create their own, official-looking documents. Sometimes they just pressed foreign coins onto an ink pad, then onto their own, laptop generated documents, purposely smearing the "seal" to give it that bureaucratic touch. Such improvisations and a few dollars have on occasion won over the most obstinate border guards at isolated crossings, but this strategy can backfire with disastrous consequences, like fines or imprisonment. Baum and Knox were fortunate not to get caught; we recommend following the rules.

Press Accreditation
Formal press credentials may be unnecessary in some parts of the world, but they are essential in others. Countries typically require foreign correspondents to apply for government press accreditation, even if they work in that country only temporarily. You need to find out what the rules are ahead of time, and how they apply to freelancers. Although requirements vary from country to country, they generally include a letter of authorization from a legitimate news outlet, your passport number, and passport photos. Most embassies and consulates have information about accreditation, or can help you find it. Some countries make it easy on foreign reporters, and some don't.

The Spanish government, for instance, presents a classic catch-22 when it comes to press accreditation. The Prime Minister's press office typically will not grant accreditation to a freelancer until he or she has obtained working papers and proof of residency. But generally you cannot obtain working papers without proof of residency. And guess what? You can't get residency unless you have working papers. It's plenty confusing, even for Spanish civil servants whose job it is to uphold the rules.

In central Asia, the accreditation requirements reflect the region's political history. "It's the former Soviet Union, and they behave like Soviets," Steve LeVine said. An official press credential from each of the various republics is essential if you plan to freelance there, especially if you hope to interview government officials.

According to LeVine, foreign reporters can't get accreditation through the mail or over the phone; most officials in these countries insist that journalists apply in person at the appropriate ministry after arrival. In general, they also require that the publication or broadcaster you string for send a fax requesting accreditation—on official letterhead—directly to them; a second letter describing the news outlet and the size of its audience; a third letter describing you and your qualifications; and several passport photos. Even then, according to LeVine, accreditation is not guaranteed: these decisions are made at the whim of a "media committee" controlled by the former KGB.

Bangkok-based Daniel Pruzin discovered that Thailand's application procedures for press accreditation, a work permit, and a yearly resident visa—three necessary items—"are ludicrously complicated and time-consuming." Officially, freelancers are not allowed to work in Thailand or other Southeast Asian countries such as Vietnam, said Pruzin.

Countries that make accreditation difficult tend to be those without a tradition of free speech. Governments there are often hostile to journalists, especially foreign freelancers who are frequently perceived as semi-employed troublemakers.

Authoritarian governments usually don't like freelancers because they consider them to be unaccountable. Sure, governments can expel individual freelancers they don't like, said one producer at a major radio network, but an image-conscious government would much prefer to shape coverage by threatening to withhold accreditation from entire media organizations.

FOLLOWING THE RULES

A lack of accreditation may prevent you from attending official news conferences, briefings, and receiving official press releases. But don't worry if you fail to meet the official accreditation requirements. There's usually a way around them, except in tightly controlled countries like China. Again, it is advisable to find out the rules over the phone, without giving your name. Then, if you decide to bend the rules, nobody in the consulate or embassy should be the wiser about your subsequent application for a tourist or student visa. It is generally not a good idea to break rules, particularly in countries with authoritarian governments. However, following the rules might make your job impossible. The circumstances and your best judgment should point the way.

From 1992 through 1994, LeVine filed from Russia to *Newsweek* and other major media while accredited through the *Lahore Friday Times*, an obscure weekly in northeast Pakistan. The editor, a friend of LeVine's from the days when he covered fighting in Afghanistan, requested accreditation for LeVine as a favor. Eventually, LeVine was accredited for *Newsweek*, but only after serious schmoozing with the Foreign Ministry functionary assigned to review his request. *USA Today*'s Elisa Tinsley had a similar experience, freelancing for a year in what was then the Soviet Union while awaiting proper accreditation. "The Foreign Ministry kept me hanging," she said. "Why? It's Kremlinology."

Al Goodman, too, worked around the rules, reporting for a few years in Spain while officially accredited as a full-time foreign correspondent for the *Wine Spectator*, a New York–based magazine for wine connoisseurs. It's true that Goodman sipped wine with Spanish nobles and jet-set vintners, but not full time. He worked primarily for other, mainstream media. The Prime Minister's press office, aware of his other work, chose to ignore the situation.

Once, Goodman stopped by the press office to drop off a copy of the *Wine Spectator* for a certain senior official. But a sharp-eyed aide noticed that the article Goodman had written about Spanish wines clearly identified him as a freelancer. She kindly suggested that he hold onto the magazine. Goodman thanked her politely, quickly put the magazine in his briefcase, and walked out the door. Later, he received proper accreditation as a freelance correspondent for CNN and *The New York Times*, as well as the accompanying work permits and residency card.

Keep in mind that government bureaucrats are not necessarily at liberty to tell you anything but the official policy, even if the rules are not enforced. Therefore, the best people to ask about the reality of accreditation requirements in a particular country are foreign reporters already on the ground there.

You could investigate the issue when contacting the AP or Reuters bureau in your destination country, or try the foreign press club there. Ask the following questions: is accreditation necessary? What are the requirements? Are freelancers eligible? How, when, and where should one apply? How long does the process take? For how long is such accreditation valid? Getting at least some of the answers before you go will give you a head start, and should help you avoid unwelcome complications later.

The solution to many accreditation problems is a letter from one of your media outlets, on letterhead, vouching for you as a stringer. But persuading editors and producers to assist in the accreditation process is often frustrating, as many are reluctant to go to bat for you, even after you've actually proven your ability abroad. "There are too many people already out there misrepresenting themselves," said the *Miami Herald*'s Juan Tamayo, citing the time he applied for accreditation in Moscow

only to be told that the *Miami Herald* already had a corr
dent accredited there—somebody whose name Tamayo didn't
even recognize.

Similarly, *The Christian Science Monitor*'s Clayton Jones recalled the case of a *Monitor* staff reporter who applied for accreditation in Cambodia. "The official laughed, and told the
reporter: 'We've had thirteen other applications from people
who said they're from the *Monitor*.'"

Because of this, you might have to postpone official accreditation, enter a country on a tourist visa, start working, and then
persuade your media contacts to write the necessary letters.

> ***Important Tip:*** Proper press credentials are a must in
> war zones, where journalists are sometimes mistaken for
> spies. In the former Yugoslavia, for example, reporters
> carry a standard press credential issued by Western
> peace-keeping forces. For further guidance on working
> in combat areas, read chapter 6: War Zone, and contact
> the Committee to Protect Journalists (see appendix 2:
> Sources and Contacts).

Alternate Accreditation Strategies

Regardless of government press accreditation abroad, you
should plan on bringing a press pass with you. One good option is the freelancer's press pass issued by the National Writers Union. This laminated photo ID is worth the price of
annual union dues, which vary according to your freelance income. This pass will prove adequate in virtually all circumstances, and is available by contacting: NWU, UAW Local 1981,
listed in appendix 2.

Another option is a generic letter of introduction from various editors for whom you will be working. Editors may be persuaded, on a case-by-case basis, to write a brief "To whom it
may concern" letter on official letterhead, verifying your status
as a stringer and requesting all necessary access to news sites

and cooperation from local authorities. This is different than a letter to a foreign government requesting official accreditation.

In the end, it may turn out that press credentials are rarely used in a given country, except for access to government press conferences and other state functions. In many countries, you can enter a government building for an interview simply by showing a passport, business card, or NWU press pass.

That worked for John Pollack, who reported for almost three years from Spain on a tourist visa, without submitting the requisite government paperwork. The Spanish Prime Minister's press office, responsible for accreditation and with which Pollack dealt regularly, simply looked the other way. Similarly, Steve LeVine found official accreditation to be unnecessary in both the Philippines and Pakistan. (If you plan on heading to these countries, check requirements before you go; conditions may have changed.)

Ditto in Thailand, where Daniel Pruzin found that many freelancers enter on a tourist visa or three-month nonimmigrant visa. The only problem with this approach is its inconvenience: you have to leave the country every three months to get a new visa.

In assessing accreditation, consider what kinds of stories you will be filing. It may help you decide whether or not to pursue an official press pass. If travel and cooking are your main topics, then government documents may not be worth the bother. Accreditation is much more important if you will be writing about national politics and perhaps drawing the attention of government officials. It all depends on the country or countries where you plan to work. Keep in mind that even with an official press pass you can still get in trouble. Russian and Uzbek officials expelled freelancer Steve LeVine from their countries after he had been working there two years. The Uzbeks complained that his reports were too critical of their government; the Russians' reasons were never clear at all.

GETTING THE RIGHT EQUIPMENT

In World War I, a resourceful Reuters correspondent used carrier pigeons to file his dispatches to London from the bloody battlefields of Europe. In later years, competing correspondents in exotic locales would dash with the latest news to what was usually a foreign city's only available telex machine; the reporter who got there first scooped the others, forcing them to wait in line, tapping their feet and swearing profusely as the precious minutes ticked by.

Today, technology has democratized the process of filing stories from abroad. In most situations, inexpensive computers and the proliferation of sophisticated telecommunications give almost all correspondents access to the outside world in a matter of minutes, even seconds. But you need the right equipment.

"The days when you could just show up in a country with your typewriter and start filing are over," former *New York Times* Moscow correspondent Philip Taubman told John Pollack in 1990, as Pollack weighed moving to Spain. Recalling those pre-laptop days, William Montalbano of the *Los Angeles Times* noted that you could pick out the foreign correspondents in any airport by the ubiquitous black typewriter cases they invariably lugged about.

Fortunately, the necessary high-tech equipment is getting more efficient, more portable, and cheaper all the time. Precisely because it is developing so quickly, however, it is difficult to recommend specific technology. The following, however, is a list of the basic gear a freelance foreign correspondent will need in order to set up shop abroad.

- **Laptop computer.** Slim laptop computers are today's equivalent of yesteryear's bulky Smith-Corona typewriters. A good, powerful laptop will pay for itself time and time again.

They are also inconspicuous, reducing the likelihood of theft or unwelcome attention from airport customs officials. Skip the typical nylon and Velcro carrying case that screams "Hey there, thieves and customs officials! Look at my nifty, hi-tech goodies!" Travel instead with your laptop in a plain, padded, canvas shoulder bag.

In selecting a laptop, buy a major brand with a warranty, preferably from a manufacturer that has an authorized service center in your target country. Finding a dealer to service an obscure brand abroad is a sure-fire exercise in frustration. Remember to purchase the correct plug and voltage adapter for your destination, and carry the purchase receipt.

Having done things the hard way, Ann Marsh suggests buying a laptop well in advance of moving abroad, so that you have enough time to get used to it and trouble-shoot any startup bugs with technical help nearby. "I gave myself only a month between deciding to go and leaving. I unknowingly bought a computer with a bad hard disk from a no-name company that went out of business a few years later. Big mistake. Combine that with the horrid phone connections to Central Europe, and I'm lucky I had such patient editors. Often, I resorted to printing out stories and faxing them from Prague's central post office late at night."

Steve LeVine first went abroad when Radio Shack's primitive laptops were considered Cadillacs. His worked well until the day he set the computer on the edge of an open fifty-five-gallon water drum while using the bathroom at the AP's Manila Bureau. Although the drum cramped movement in the small room, AP staffers relied on it for scoop showers in times of low water pressure. LeVine, washing his hands in the sink, accidentally knocked the laptop into the barrel. Though he grabbed it before it hit bottom, the word processor never worked again. LeVine's father had to ship him a replacement, which set him back a thousand dollars.

Dan DeLuce, heading for Czechoslovakia to start his ca-

reer as a foreign correspondent, had to switch train
middle of the night somewhere in Germany. Dr
duffel bag down the grimy, dimly lit platforr
he'd arrived on pulled away from the stat'
denly struck by a pang of mortifying h⌐   .ew
$2,000 laptop was still tucked und   ⌐ train,
where he'd hidden it for safekeᵉ   .ozed. Desperate, DeLuce started to run, l   1ate. The train
disappeared into the night and hi∟   ⌐ was gone forever.
And he hadn't even reached his final ⌐estination.

With these incidents in mind, buy a good laptop; it will
save you time and aggravation. And take care of it. A moment of carelessness can wreak havoc on your savings, your
stories, and your sanity.

- **Fax/modem**. Buy this with your laptop, and invest in quality. Your fax/modem will be your laptop's link with the outside world. You will use it to send and receive faxes, file
  stories, and exchange e-mail messages. An internal fax/
  modem is best because it eliminates the inconvenience of
  tangled cords, batteries, and multiple adapters that often accompany externally mounted models. Practice using your
  fax/modem before you go.

- **Software.** Word-processing software is essential, along with
  a web browser and communications software to operate
  your fax/modem. You also should investigate access to the
  Internet in your destination and buy any software necessary to conveniently utilize these services. With the right
  on-line provider you'll be able to read wire stories in real
  time, keeping abreast of breaking news related to your region. Major service providers or computer consultants at
  most universities should be able to help you find out how to
  connect overseas, since the Internet has become the preferred means of rapid communication in the global academic village. If you can't figure it out before departing, inquire

at a local university or computer store (if one exists) after you arrive.

With increasing frequency, media want their freelancers to file via e-mail or through private networks using a local overseas access number. Access to the Internet will give you more options and likely prove the most cost-effective means of international communication.

Advertising Age, a Crain Communications publication with active stringers in about seventy-five countries worldwide, tries to provide its freelancers with communications software at the outset, because the publication relies heavily on e-mail links. "Communication is constant," said Jan Jaben, its international editor. "We give assignments on e-mail. It's much more convenient. I couldn't imagine living without e-mail."

- **Printer.** Buy the most portable printer possible, because you might be on the road regularly. Although your fax/modem will obviate the need for a lot of printing, you will inevitably need to print some correspondence. The quality should be good enough for business letters, but does not need to be laser quality. Some newer laptops are equipped with built-in printers beneath the keyboard. Carry extra ink cartridges, even though computer supplies are becoming more common throughout Europe, Asian capitals, and in other major cities around the world.

  Warning: do not buy a printer that requires special paper, and make sure that it can handle sheets of various widths, because standards vary around the world.

- **Camera.** Professional photographers will shudder at the suggestion, but modern camera technology gives even amateur photographers the ability to shoot photos quite adequate to accompany most articles. If you have a fancy camera with lots of lenses, fine. But any decent point-and-shoot camera with built-in flash and zoom lens will do, and it will pay for itself with two or three pictures. Photos help sell stories, especially features, and can generate hundreds of dollars extra in annual income. Be sure to purchase backup batteries and a modest supply of film, which typically costs more abroad. If you buy a digital camera, make sure it can interface with your laptop.

• **Tape recorder.** If you do not plan to string for radio networks, a small hand-held recorder should be enough. Make sure the built-in microphone can be pointed toward the speaker at the same time you can see the tape counter, to help you keep track of important quotes during interviews. Other good features are a pause button and tape-speed control.

If you plan to file radio spots, consult your likely clients about recommended equipment. National Public Radio engineer Dennis Byrnes suggested the following: a portable digital audio (DAT) deck; an omnidirectional microphone; audio adapters and an assortment of microphone cables; a mono-line amplifier to boost sound going to a standard or satellite telephone; a 14- to 16-inch "shotgun" mike and a flexible six-foot extension pole to put it on; and a padded bag to carry it all.

Some of this gear may not be necessary if your target country can install an Integrated Services Digital Network (ISDN) phone line at your home or office. ISDN lines transmit studio-quality sound, a vast improvement over the raspy, crackling phone lines that are all too common in many foreign countries. Depending on your skills, you might consider buying software that enables you to edit complete radio packages on your laptop, as if you were in a studio. Such software lets the correspondent mix sound bites, ambient sound, and the reporter's voice tracks without a second tape deck and without sending a report's sound elements back to the studio separately for editing. You can record voice tracks directly into the laptop if your computer has the proper port for an external microphone (built-in mikes usually are inadequate for producing professional-quality radio sound). Afterward, you can transmit the entire package to the studio, broadcast-ready.

After Al Goodman had been stringing for NPR for several months, his producer arranged for him to buy professional gear from NPR's discount supplier. Radio stringers should ask their networks up front about that kind of assistance.

As with laptops, buying major-brand radio equipment is safer than settling for discount models because major brands are easier to service abroad. Dan Baum and Margaret Knox were in northern Madagascar when their Sony PCM 5000 conked out. They had been filing to NPR, BBC, and the Australian Broadcasting Corporation, tapping into phone lines with alligator clips. "It was so primitive," Baum said. "Our stuff always sounded like we were reporting from the dark side of the moon." When their tape recorder stopped working, they resigned themselves to pursuing only print stories for the rest of the trip.

But the next day, strolling through a romantic, lost-in-time colonial neighborhood in Antsirane amidst rickshaws and barefoot townsfolk, they suddenly came upon a modern stereo shop with a JVC sign in the window. "It was as if God put this stereo shop in this remote spot just so we could have our deck fixed," Baum said. For the equivalent of $9, they were back in business.

- **Telephone/answering machine.** Many countries have antiquated phone systems with archaic instruments. Bringing a push-button phone with both pulse and tone capability, automatic re-dial, and a built-in answering machine will enable you to set up a home office efficiently and economically. Memory dialing for a dozen or more frequently used numbers is also a time-saving feature, and a headset attachment can save you a sore neck. If the phone uses electrical current, be sure to get the correct adapter for your target country.

- **Digital phone directory.** This or a paper equivalent is a big help in organizing contact names and phone numbers.

- **Phone cord.** Make sure your cord is long, has two male ends, and bring a female phone jack for attachment to phone lines. This will enable you to transmit information more easily in poorly equipped apartments or hotel rooms. As late as 1993 Madrid's Palace Hotel, a luxurious monument to Beaux Arts opulence catering to the world's top foreign correspondents, lacked modern phone jacks. Bring a small screwdriver, alligator clips, and electrical tape to attach the new jack to the old phone line. Alligator clips, named for their jawlike form, are available at electronics and hardware stores. Using them to connect the jack and phone line is simple: just clip them to the wires inside the jack and line (you may have to unscrew the small phone plug box on the wall), matching the wires by color. To avoid frustration, practice the procedure when you're not on deadline.

  The purchase of a conventional phone may not be necessary if you are confident your housing overseas will come with one, or if you plan on buying a conventional or mobile phone in your destination country. Still, you may want both, because mobile phones are often uncomfortable to wedge between your ear and shoulder while taking notes during a phone interview, not to mention their penchant for malfunctioning.

- **Short-wave radio with AM/FM bands.** Buy a portable model with a built-in alarm clock. This allows you to listen to the local news, BBC World Service, and the Voice of America, among others. Bring an earplug or headphones and extra batteries. If your short-wave radio won't fit in your pocket, consider buying another palm-sized AM-FM radio. It will enable you to listen to the local news while on the move, a good way to keep abreast of breaking developments.

If you're planning to freelance abroad for television as a correspondent, producer, or camera operator, you should plan on renting equipment in your target region. New, basic Betacam gear (camera, tripod, lights, microphones, editing deck, etc.) can cost $60,000 to $150,000—not the kind of investment to consider when you're just starting out. To complicate matters, American crews use NTSC-format Betacam cameras, while in Europe the standard is PAL.

You might consider taking a smaller Hi-8 camera, even if you don't plan to work in television. If you see breaking news and happen to be the only person to shoot it on camera, your Hi-8 images might be very salable to TV networks for a hefty fee, perhaps thousands of dollars.

Important Tip: Before shopping for these items, find out the current, voltage, and type of plug that are standard in your destination. Worldwide, there are fifty varieties of plug-socket combinations, twenty in Europe alone, according to the *International Herald Tribune*. The United States, Canada, and Japan adhere to a 110-volt standard for household power, while most of the world runs on 220 volts. Appliances in the U.S. feature two flat prongs; those in some western European countries feature two round prongs, while in England plugs have three prongs (see Foreign Electricity Guide, page 185).

Be aware that plug adapters that enable you to plug appliances into foreign outlets are usually only part of the equation: you also need to adapt the voltages. Many new computers come with AC adapters that work for both American and European standards, but check with the manufacturer to see what is required. The last thing you want to do is fry your new laptop, as freelancer Ann

Marsh did when she plugged hers in without an adapter her first day in Paris. It also happened to a CNN sports crew with a video editing deck at the 1992 Barcelona Olympics. If in doubt, don't plug in.

This is the basic list. Other equipment, such as first aid kits, water purification filters, and body armor may be necessary for work in remote or dangerous environments. For more information about such situations, see chapter 6: War Zone.

In the final analysis, getting the right equipment will make your job easier, but it won't do the work for you. The main equipment you need is your brain.

FINANCIAL, MEDICAL, AND OTHER LOGISTICAL PREPARATIONS

There are several other preparations that will help smooth your transition abroad, and financial considerations top the list. Based on your budget calculations from the previous chapter, allocate enough money to support yourself without income for at least three months, perhaps more if moving to a crowded news hub. Shortly before departure, divide your money into traveler's checks and cash. The exact amount of each depends on where you're going. Traveler's checks and cash should be in U.S. dollars, British pounds, or another hard currency. Be sure to bring lots of small bills if you are heading to out-of-the-way places. If you want to give a tip—or a bribe— don't expect the person to make change.

Credit Cards

If you don't have one already, get a credit card. Your credit limit should be high enough to cover at least a month or two of activity. Make sure that the monthly bills are sent to an address where you will be apprised of them quickly and can pay them off without delay. Ideally, you will enlist a friend, family member, or colleague to provide such logistical support at home.

If you plan on working in a foreign country for some time, you may want to take advantage of the overseas toll-free or collect phone numbers that credit card issuers now provide so their cardholders can get up-to-date account information. In Spain, for example, Al Goodman calls collect or toll-free each month through AT&T's USA Direct to reach his credit card and AT&T calling card accounts. He finds out the balance due, gets an itemized list of the charges, and then sends—from Spain—a check drawn on his U.S. bank to pay the bill. While the payment is heading toward the United States, arriving on time, the actual printed bill is being sent to him in Spain. Increasingly, many of these inquiries can be completed via computer, too.

Credit cards also allow you to get cash advances at overseas automatic teller machines or in foreign banks. Keep in mind that this type of transaction does not work in every country, even when it is touted to be automatic. That's why you should always have some "walking-around" money. Check with the company that issues your card for details. Ask your current bank for advice on transferring funds abroad, because traditional bank transfers and money wires are not always speedy and can carry hefty commissions or service charges.

International Calling Cards
In addition to a credit card, get a telephone calling card that is valid for calls from abroad. Check with major carriers beforehand to make sure they provide service from your target country or region. Again, have the bills sent to an address where you will be apprised of them in a timely manner and inquire about the overseas collect numbers for the carrier's cardholders. Mail overseas can be notoriously slow, so plan accordingly.

Health Insurance
Health insurance is another important consideration. Check with your current insurer to determine if your policy is valid

abroad, and if so, for how long. Canadian and British citizens may not need to worry so much about this, but Americans cannot be too careful. Special insurance may be needed if you plan to work in a war zone; see chapter 6 for detailed information.

If you are not covered or are looking for a more affordable plan, inquire about membership in and health insurance through American Citizens Abroad, a very helpful organization based in Switzerland (see appendix 2: Sources and Contacts).

As a young freelancer without health insurance in 1970, Alan Riding landed in a Mexican hospital after a large truck totaled his Volkswagen Beetle. "It cleaned out my entire account. I was down to bare bones," he said. Riding considers himself lucky, though. "If the truck had been loaded with stones I would have been bits and pieces. It would not have been an auspicious three-month career."

Aware of such dangers, Nick Anderson—who freelanced for a year in Mexico City before The Associated Press hired him there in 1996—initially chose a COBRA health plan that permitted him to continue the comprehensive health coverage he enjoyed as a reporter at the *San Jose Mercury News*. "It cost— ugh, painful to remember it—$137 per month," he said. After meeting another freelancer with a high-deductible plan costing only $50 per month, he switched policies. "For small stuff, I'll pay out of pocket," he said.

Prescription Drugs
If you take prescription drugs, get your prescriptions filled before leaving and ask a reputable pharmacist about finding refills abroad. If the drugs have a long shelf life, consider telling your doctor and/or the pharmacist that you are going to be overseas for an extended period and need all the refills at once to take with you. Try to determine ahead of time the rules about bringing medical supplies into your target country. Embassy officials may be of help.

If vaccinations are necessary, get them while you're still on your home turf, and find out when—and under what conditions—you have to repeat them. In India, for example, Terin Miller brought his own needles and syringes, along with rubbing alcohol, to be revaccinated safely by local health care professionals who had the skills and training to give injections, but lacked adequate medical supplies.

Bank Accounts

It's a good idea to maintain a bank account in your home country where your media clients can send checks or wire payments. You will get paid faster and probably lose less in exchange commissions. In addition, you may not want or be allowed to open a foreign bank account, especially if you lack proper working and residency papers. Ask your hometown bank if it would be willing to receive and deposit checks and to notify you regularly by mail or e-mail of your account activity. You can access this cash abroad via credit cards or wire transfers. Once you arrive overseas and make a few inquiries, however, you may want to open a local bank account.

A CRASH COURSE IN LANGUAGE AND CULTURE

Staff foreign correspondents for major media can readily fly into most countries and, if necessary, hire a translator at company expense. By contrast, freelancers need to learn the local language, both for professional and economic reasons. Translators are often expensive, and speaking the local language gives freelancers a vital competitive advantage. Learning it should be a top priority, no matter how exotic or difficult it might seem at first.

"Even when you're dealing with easy languages, the guy who speaks fluent French or Spanish is going to be ahead of the guy who doesn't," Alan Riding said. Keep the example of Lawrence

Sheets in mind: he got his start as a foreign correspondent almost entirely because of his fluency in Russian. He had honed his skills semester after laborious semester in college, even spending two summers in what was then Leningrad, one in a small communal apartment above a seedy beer hall with nine other Russians and more than a couple of rats. He did it because he found Russian and the Soviet Union intriguing.

Not everyone will have the language skills Sheets did when he set off, though it may be unrealistic to expect to become truly functional in a foreign language before living in that country. But learning the basics before you go is eminently possible wherever you find yourself. The words *please, thank you, hello,* and *good-bye* should be rolling off your tongue long before your departure. Your goal is to be able to gather information and conduct an effective interview in that language. Try to take a language course ahead of time. Even if you don't have time to study formally, buy a good introductory text, dictionary, and phrase book in the language you will need and pack them for use after arrival. Language tapes, if they are available from your public library or local bookstore, can also be very helpful. After you arrive overseas, listening to local television or radio can sharpen your skills quickly.

Of course, it is possible to work as a correspondent in a country where you don't speak the language, and situations will arise when you'll have to get by with English, a translator, or some other form of communication. "Language is important, but if you have really good journalism skills, that can compensate for everything," said *USA Today*'s Elisa Tinsley. Ultimately, though, your opportunities as a freelance journalist abroad will depend on your communication skills. If you want to work for the major media, you had better learn the local language.

Knowing as much as you can about the history, politics, and culture of your destination is also extremely important. Without context, your stories will lack color and depth, and you will have a harder time selling them. So in the months or weeks before your departure, read as much as you can related to your destination. Take advantage of books, magazines, newspapers, television, radio, CDs, and other resources dealing with your target country. From this material, cull a few selected reference resources to take with you. A good general history book is helpful, and so is a detailed paperback atlas of the world. Many resources are now available on-line, and can be stored electronically on your laptop's hard drive. The disadvantage of such storage is that you're unlikely to browse through it while riding the train, waiting for a bus, or drinking a beer in a streetside café. Books still top computers when it comes to dependability: you can step on a book, get it wet, dry it out, and usually leave it in plain sight without worry of theft. And, unlike a hard drive, it won't crash if you drop it.

Whatever your approach may be to educating yourself, be sure you know the basics about your region before your departure, and plan on becoming an expert in the months after your arrival.

FINDING A CHEAP TICKET

Try to fly directly to your destination without overnight stopovers that drive up ticket prices, drain your financial resources and test your nerves. Shop around for tickets. Ask travel agents about various departure dates and airlines, because they're unlikely to volunteer information regarding cheap deals. Tickets from consolidators are usually less expensive than those from ordinary travel agents or those purchased directly from the airlines. In addition, take advantage of promotions featured in the Sunday travel sections of major metropolitan dailies.

Al Goodman can personally attest to the importance of flying directly to one's destination, because he chose not to in 1987 and got off to a terrible start. Goodman and his girlfriend, an

English teacher, were headed to Madrid but instead took a flight from Chicago via New York to Paris, where Goodman wanted to visit a friend. For starters, the airline lost his girl-friend's luggage. It finally showed up several days later as they boarded a train from Paris to Madrid. But because it was peak tourist season and they hadn't reserved tickets on the express train, they were stuck on a slow-moving local. That meant maddening stops in the middle of nowhere, then switching trains in the dead of night at the French-Spanish border, haul-ing heavy suitcases. It was a wonder Goodman made it to Madrid; his girlfriend wanted to dump him at the border.

Open-ended round-trip tickets are often valid for up to a year; try to get one. This gives you the comfort of knowing you can go home when you wish and it will also deter questions from border guards who often demand proof that you will be leaving the country. Even if you plan to stay abroad indefi-nitely, you will likely want a vacation at home eventually.

Round-trip tickets purchased in such competitive markets as the United States or Great Britain usually are cheaper than those bought in many other nations. One-way tickets typically end up costing more money.

Finally, try to be flexible about your departure date. Some-times the difference of waiting a day or a week before taking off can save you a lot of cash.

When packing your bags, aim to travel as lightly as possible. You do not want to look like a roving high-tech store. Carry on your laptop and other delicate electronics, and pack the rest in ordinary luggage. As a general rule, don't bring more luggage than you yourself can comfortably handle. Try moving your luggage at home, before you have to rush for the airport. If you can't handle the luggage by yourself, consider leaving things behind, or purchasing a portable luggage cart to boost your ca-pacity.

> ***Important Tip:*** Your arrival may run more smoothly if you aim to land in a pleasant season. It's obviously harder to travel in snow, heavy rain, or broiling heat. Also, be sure to check on local holidays: Are you scheduled to arrive in the middle of the nation's weeklong annual festival, when everything is closed? Or during the summer holiday, when everybody is on vacation?

ENTERING THE RING

As your day of departure approaches, you will probably be nervous, perhaps even terrified. That's natural. Becoming a freelance foreign correspondent is a big challenge, one filled with excitement and uncertainty. If moving abroad were a casual endeavor, everybody would do it. That you have the guts to try it indicates you have the potential to succeed. And with potential, anything is possible.

Relevant here is an old Spanish saying: *¡Adelante, vista, y al toro!*

The phrase is derived from a tradition that foreign correspondent and author Ernest Hemingway considered a window into the human character: bullfighting. Loosely translated, the phrase says, "Onward! Look ahead, and face the bull!" But you don't have to be a bullfighting aficionado to appreciate its deeper meaning. The words speak to risk, courage, and rising to the challenges that confront us in life. They speak also to passion, fate, clarity of vision, and—when the moment arrives—to casting aside doubtful procrastination. The old saying compresses all of these elements into a single moment, a moment of departure. Yours is such a moment.

4 STRANGER IN A FOREIGN LAND

he Spain of John Pollack's imagination was broad and dusty, a sunny land of ruined castles and crowded bullfights, of red wine and flamenco and the stubborn ghost of a dead dictator stirring up trouble.

The Spain he discovered was all of that, and much more. By 1991 the country had become Europe's economic upstart. Work was moving full tilt on new roads and buildings for the Olympics in Barcelona, the World's Fair in Seville, and the high-speed rail link between Madrid and Seville. Five centuries after Columbus encountered the New World, Spain was consciously grooming itself for center stage once again, and planning 1992 as a yearlong coming-out party.

As an aspiring foreign correspondent, Pollack planned to write about it all, saying *adiós* to Plainville datelines forever! But as his plane dropped through the gray clouds over Madrid, the nagging doubts he had struggled to keep at bay welled through him like a brackish spring.

Pollack knew he faced an enormous challenge, and was plenty nervous. He was hoping like hell to avoid inspection of his luggage, because he hadn't been able to get a work visa before leaving and was carrying a new laptop computer, printer, and résumés—not exactly the belongings of a typical tourist. If challenged, he was ready to tell half the truth: that he was a re-porter on vacation. Given his limited Spanish, it seemed like a plausible story.

Pollack needn't have worried. After a long wait in line, the border guard stamped his passport with a cursory glance, and the Civil Guards—some cradling submachine guns—waved him through without an inspection.

Good luck ended there. Sensing Pollack's unfamiliarity with Spain, the taxi driver charged him triple for the trip into Madrid, a city that at first seemed a noisy metropolis of ugly apartment blocks, all choked in winter smog. Pollack was so green he even gave the guy a big tip.

Setting off to become a foreign correspondent had seemed so daring when he was poring over the oversized *National Geographic Atlas* in the comfort of his parents' living room in Ann Arbor, Pollack recalled. But two hours after landing—standing beside his bags on the dirty curb of an unfamiliar street, the chairs and tables of its sidewalk cafés stacked and chained—he found the situation incredibly intimidating.

Ignorant of Spain's culinary delicacies and worried about his wallet, Pollack ate greasy bar food for dinner that day, then discovered a nearby 7-Eleven selling Oscar Mayer wieners and the Spanish equivalent of Wonder Bread. Though he had arranged to stay temporarily in the vacant apartment of a family acquaintance, the landlord had turned off the gas. So the kitchen was inoperable except for an electric kettle, which would blow the fuse and plunge the apartment into darkness whenever his hot dogs approached lukewarm.

After a few days had passed, Pollack realized that a terrible exchange rate was taking its toll on his thinning cache of traveler's checks. He had about $1,800 to carry him until he found work, a sum that wasn't going to last long in a European capital. Everything seemed terribly expensive; daily newspapers cost the equivalent of a dollar, coffee came in tiny cups—no refills—and his high school Spanish wasn't even good enough to complain.

Historic Madrid? He had to concentrate on the sidewalk: there was dog crap everywhere. Financially and emotionally, the meter was running fast. His confidence wavered. Just how soon could he fly home and still save face?

In retrospect, Pollack's landing in Spain went relatively smoothly. Dan Baum and Margaret Knox—heading for Zimbabwe—decided to fly into Nairobi, Kenya, then hitchhike the final 1,500 miles to "get a sense of what Africa was really like."

Gung-ho from the very start, Baum and Knox eschewed the regular $3 airport bus to downtown Nairobi, instead jostling their way onto the crowded local bus. The fare? Only three cents each. But it was an expensive trip. Despite their money belts and vigilance, a pickpocket lifted Baum's wallet, passport, vaccination card, $100 in Kenyan shillings, and his American Express card.

Horrified to discover their loss, they made a frustrating stop at the police department, then made their way to a cheap, dingy hotel, checked into a room, and locked the door. It was hot and stuffy. Traffic noise and the smell of fried food permeated the air. Knox lay down on the bed. Baum went to the window and flung it open, only to be enveloped in a sudden belch of diesel exhaust from a passing truck. "You want Africa?" he exclaimed. "There it is, Meg!"

Without question, getting started is the hardest part of becoming a freelance foreign correspondent. Many would-be correspondents end up heading home prematurely, casualties of unrealistic expectations, failing to tackle their challenge in a systematic way or falling prey to crippling blunders with resident correspondents. Generally, luck is not a determining factor in one's success abroad. Dogged persistence is. By following a few simple guidelines and using a systematic approach to develop contacts and generate work, talented new arrivals can generally become working foreign correspondents in a matter of months.

Or days. Less than 24 hours after arriving, Baum and Knox made their way to The Associated Press bureau, where a sympathetic reporter told them that the BBC needed a stringer right away for a Q and A about a speech just delivered by Kenya's president. The AP reporter gave a crash briefing on the speech and its significance, then Baum got on the phone with a BBC anchor in London. Hours later, Baum and Knox, out on the street with their short-wave radio, listened to the interview. It sounded good. Africa was okay, after all.

When landing in a new country, the best attitude may be to expect the unexpected. Laura Ballman left the United States for Kiev, anxious to begin her new job as features editor at *Intel News*, a daily English-language newsletter sent to embassies and businesses in the Ukraine. But the day she arrived, her job was cut; *Intel News* no longer needed a features editor. Ballman stayed on as a features reporter, and hustled to line up other work. Soon she was stringing for CBS Radio and UPI.

FIRST THINGS FIRST: FINDING A PLACE TO LIVE AND WORK

As in any move to a new city, finding a place to live is a top priority. This is particularly true for freelancers, who will probably be working out of their homes. Low overhead is key to successful freelancing, and a home/office—even if only a single room in a shared apartment—will help stretch critical resources. Getting settled as soon as possible after arrival is important; it will help provide both a sense of belonging and an economical base of operations from which to launch your new business. Even if you plan to cover a broad region and travel a lot, a home base is essential.

John Pollack, after a search through the Madrid classified ads and dozens of fruitless phone calls, found a spare room in the apartment of two immigrants from the Dominican Republic. Todd Bensman, moving to Prague for his second foray abroad, ended up living with a Czech family for about $50 per month. Steve LeVine, landing in the Philippines, set up shop in Manila's equivalent of Motel 6, renting a room for about $150 per month.

Finding the right place can take time. If you don't have a free bed lined up before arriving, check into a budget hotel or hostel, give yourself a day to get over jet lag if necessary, and begin the housing search right away. Although personal taste varies and differences in geography, culture, and economics preclude the possibility of offering detailed housing advice on a country-by-country or city-by-city basis, the following guidelines are generally applicable worldwide.

- Rent cheap when you are getting started, allocating no more than 30 percent of your projected income. Move into fancier digs later, if your income permits. Here are some house-hunting tips:

  1. Newspapers and circulars advertising rental property and second-hand goods are available in many foreign cities. Consult these publications the morning they appear on newsstands, and follow up on leads immediately.

  2. Check universities, English-language bookstores, and other expatriate hangouts for bulletin boards featuring "room for rent" fliers.

  3. Ask your country's consulate or embassy for housing suggestions. Although embassy personnel typically live well beyond the means of novice freelancers, they may know of spare rooms for rent or potential house-sitting clients.

  4. Identify neighborhoods you can afford to live in, then walk the streets seeking "for rent" signs. Ask local merchants or doormen at apartment buildings about nearby apartments or rooms that may be available.

5. As a last resort only, consider enlisting the help of a rental agency. However, these are often outrageously expensive.

• A telephone is the single most important tool in any reporter's home office. Whether you have a private line or share a phone, a telephone is your link to both news and news outlets. Do not move into a place that does not have a working telephone. Don't believe landlords who tell you it will only take a few days or a week to hook up phone service! *Mañana* can mean an eternity. When testing the phone, check for modern phone jacks that facilitate easy connection of your modem and answering machine. Although they are not essential, these jacks can save time and minimize poor connections when sending text, audio, or images to media back home. Phone lines with tone dialing, as opposed to pulse dialing, facilitate faster and better communication.

Many foreign countries still suffer under government-run communications monopolies whose poor quality is exceeded only by their terrible customer service. If you are in a country where you simply cannot find a room or apartment with a telephone, consider buying or renting a mobile phone or try locating near a public telephone exchange with pay phones and fax machines. Beeper service, if available, is another way to mitigate your isolation. In the poorest of countries, a nearby hotel may be your best option as an impromptu communications center.

• After a telephone, location is the next important consideration. In most cases, it's better to live in the heart of a major city—preferably a national capital—near government ministries, business headquarters, and cultural activities that might generate news. Living close to the city center will enable you to meet a broad variety of people and will put you in a position to be most useful to news outlets looking for a stringer.

Within that city, it is imperative to live near public transport: a bus stop, taxi stand, subway, train station, and/or airport. Ready access to public transportation will save you both time and money when they count the most. Familiarizing yourself with public transportation should be among your earliest tasks after arriving in a foreign land. Pollack erred somewhat in choosing his first apartment; it was on the outskirts of Madrid. Its telephone and proximity to the subway, however, were mitigating factors.

- When inspecting a room or apartment, check the number and location of electrical outlets, whether they are AC or DC, and their voltage. Think through your electrical needs ahead of time. How many appliances will be plugged in at once? Will using a computer, printer, and fax modem at the same time trip a circuit-breaker? Is there a circuit-breaker or fuse? Can you access it or replace fuses easily?

- Noise is an important factor to consider, especially if you need tranquility in order to write, or if you plan to record radio spots or phone in live commentary. Consider the possibilities of noise from the street, from roommates, and from neighbors. Do noise levels vary during the day? In Spain, people dine late and carouse through the streets into the wee hours. In Eastern Europe, the work day and street noise start around dawn. Factoring in time differences with your various media, when are you likely to be working most?

- Will your belongings be secure? You will likely be leaving expensive equipment in your place. A stolen laptop or tape deck can be costly to replace, especially overseas.

- Consider the lighting in the room where you will work. Light that may be adequate for social purposes may be insufficient for reading and writing. Also, are there blinds or curtains to cut down potential glare on your computer screen?

- Is the furniture adequate, or will you need to improvise? Remember that you are setting up a small business, and it's hard to stay organized on a couch or bedside table. It might be easier to rent a sparsely furnished place and then find basic furniture to meet your needs.

- Is there a television? How is the reception? Watching the local news can be an excellent way to improve your language skills, and is sometimes critical for keeping up with breaking stories. Also, does the TV receive international channels such as CNN or Sky TV? Would the landlord permit you to buy a small satellite dish and hook it up later?

- Remember to ask who pays for electricity, gas, water, or monthly payments to a building's doorman, if there is one. Seek to understand all hidden costs before signing a lease.

- Avoid signing anything other than short-term leases, if possible. News can dry up and stories can move. You might need to, as well. Remember that many landlords prefer renting to foreigners, who are likely to move on with regularity, giving them a chance to raise the rent more often than if they rented to a local. Consider using this as a bargaining chip when negotiating your rent.

- Do you like the place? Don't move into a hovel if it will make you miserable.

> ***Important Tip:*** Avoid telling prospective landlords that you are a freelance journalist. It will sound as if you don't have a regular paycheck, which is true (at first). Just say you are a reporter; or consider telling them instead what you did for a living before moving to their country, and that you have come to study the language. Most people are proud of their country and language, and this explanation may well make perfect sense to them.

NETWORKING FROM SCRATCH: HOW TO AVOID SHOOTING YOURSELF IN THE FOOT

Even as you search for housing, you should begin networking among resident journalists. The primary goal of this first round is to introduce yourself and find out who files to which media, what stories are selling, and what work might be available. If you did not ascertain which strings were available before leaving your home country, now is the time to do so. Be diplomatic about it, because new freelancers have little personal or professional capital to waste. Before embarking on this project, carefully consider the following stories.

An American freelancer showed up in Madrid on a Fulbright scholarship and almost immediately filed a radio spot to National Public Radio. His mistake? He didn't first check in with NPR's regular stringer in Madrid, Al Goodman. Weeks later, the newcomer phoned Goodman to introduce himself, casually mentioning that he had filed the spot, and proposed that they meet for coffee. An alarmed Goodman immediately sensed a turf-jumper and declined the invitation. After hanging up, Goodman called his editor on the NPR foreign desk for clarification on the situation. Yes, the newcomer had called NPR editors in Washington before coming to Spain and had been informed that Goodman was the regular NPR stringer. The editors had told the would-be stringer to expect only occasional work, if any. One busy day, harried editors on the NPR spot news desk had accepted the newcomer's 45-second news spot, over the phone, paying the standard spot fee of $30.

What most newcomers fail to recognize is that resident stringers are understandably wary of new freelance colleagues, because the newcomers are potential competition. Strings represent a freelance reporter's food and rent, and trying to steal them is considered a cardinal sin.

"If you try to move in on someone else's strings," said Todd Bensman, "that's not cool. You're messing with someone else's livelihood."

Ultimately, editors and producers are the ones who decide which freelancers to use and what to publish or broadcast. Some do call on different stringers within the same country for different types of stories. Others prefer to work with a single, reliable stringer in each location who can react effectively to breaking news and produce an accurate story quickly.

Most resident freelancers work hard to persuade editors and producers that it's best to use just one stringer who already knows the ropes. Too many stringers representing a particular news outlet in one location tend to undermine each other's local credibility, and in turn that of their client.

In the NPR incident, Goodman politely told the turf-jumper to back off. Defensive, the fellow claimed he had tried to contact Goodman before filing the radio spot, but couldn't reach him. He must not have tried too hard, because Goodman's answering machine recorded no such attempt. Soon, Goodman was cautioning others in Madrid's small freelance community to look out for their strings: a turf-jumper was in town.

Word got around. When a "local hire" reporting position opened up later at The Associated Press bureau in Madrid, Mr. Aggressive applied for the job. The bureau chief asked Pollack (already stringing for the AP) if he knew the applicant, and Pollack related the NPR incident, sparing nothing in his criticism. For whatever reason, the applicant didn't get the job.

The point is that every new correspondent needs the help and goodwill of journalists already working in that country. If you ignore this reality you shoot yourself in the foot.

Unlike Mr. Aggressive, freelance TV reporter Michael Moffett handled his arrival diplomatically. Before coming to Madrid, he called CNN in Atlanta about stringing in Spain. An editor there told him the field looked wide open. But while making other calls, Moffett heard that a guy called Al Good-man was stringing for CNN from Madrid. So Moffett called Goodman, introduced himself, and asked if Goodman would be willing to "share" the CNN string since Atlanta didn't seem to have a designated stringer. Absolutely not, Goodman replied, and suggested that Moffett call back CNN to speak with the International Desk producer in charge of overseas stringers. Moffett did, and the producer informed him that Goodman was indeed CNN's regular stringer in Spain. As Moffett discovered, one call to a newsroom isn't always enough; if you're dealing with a big organization, you also have to make sure you're talking to the right person.

Reacting quite differently to this newcomer than they did to Mr. Aggressive, resident correspondents in Spain gave Moffett plenty of good advice. He soon developed his own string with Deutsche Welle TV, a German television company that commissions English-language reports from Spain, reports that regularly air on Public Broadcasting System affiliates in the United States.

WHO'S WHO: MEETING THE PEOPLE YOU NEED TO KNOW

The people you need to meet for professional reasons generally fall into two categories: journalists and sources. Getting to know your colleagues first will save you time and effort in getting to know sources, which tend to develop over time. Make your initial contacts with English-language colleagues, then local counterparts. Start with the list of contact names, news outlets, and other organizations you compiled before departure (see chapter 3: Getting Ready to Go), calling to set up appointments. Call with confidence, introducing yourself and mentioning who, if anyone, referred you to them. Explain briefly that you are a new journalist in town who would appreciate some advice. Be succinct: the goal of this first call is only to set up a face-to-face meeting. Waste their time on the telephone, and they may not want to meet you. Offer to see them at their convenience, and let them know how to reach you if they have to cancel on short notice.

During this initial call, stress that you seek their advice, which most people like to give. Unless they ask, don't tell them right away that you're looking for a job, because it might put them off. They may well know of available work but want to size you up in person to see if you merit their help.

Begin by calling the staff correspondents, if any, of English-language newspapers, radio, and television networks who may be based in your new country. Often, these correspondents are based in neighboring countries, and are responsible for covering broad regions. Keep in mind that they might be looking for "eyes and ears" in your country, and ask to meet them the next time they come to town.

After arriving in Mexico City, Nick Anderson found quite a bit of work filling in for staffers or freelancers looking for a reliable pinch-hitter while they pursued other stories or went on vacation. "Get plugged in to the community of foreign correspondents," Anderson said. "Let them know you're out there, and they will call on you for help, because no one can run a foreign bureau all alone. Everyone needs stringers."

Try the wire services, both news and business: Associated Press, Reuters, AP–Dow Jones, Bloomberg Business News, and the occasional government-funded English-language news service. These outlets often rely on locally hired stringers to fill out their rotations, write features, or help on special projects. "As a stringer, your main advantage is your availability," said Brazilian Elena di Moura, who freelances as an international news producer for CNN in Atlanta. Stringers generally have flexible schedules and wire service bureau chiefs like to be aware of the local talent pool should openings occur. Optimally, you will have written them ahead of time to introduce yourself. Either way, an appointment with the bureau chief of The Associated Press or Reuters is one of the most important you can make.

In Manila, the AP bureau chief didn't hire Steve LeVine initially, but as a favor let the former AP staffer freelance from the office. One Friday, as the bloodless revolution against dictator Ferdinand Marcos gathered force, LeVine walked into the office and the bureau chief said, "Steve! Are you going to be busy for the coming week?" No, LeVine answered. "How'd you like to work for AP?" the bureau chief asked. LeVine was in business, a local hire for $600 per month. "It gave me credibility with all the other correspondents," LeVine said. "It gave me contacts, gave me confidence, and gave me stability."

Paid opportunities are best, but volunteering at a wire service can be a good way to get your foot in the door. Many bureau chiefs would rather not bother with interns, but if you can persuade them of your usefulness, interning can be an effective way for you to get an overview of the country, learn what's news and what's not, and position yourself for any job that opens up. Todd Bensman, who after the Gulf War volunteered in UPI's Jerusalem bureau in exchange for office space, almost parlayed his experience and the goodwill he generated into a job with UPI, covering the Kurds in Turkey. In the end, though, somebody else got the job and Bensman went broke. He decided to fly back to Alaska, where he lived out of his rusting pickup truck and gutted fish in a salmon cannery for several months until he could save enough money to drive down to the lower forty-eight, marshal his resources, and relaunch himself abroad, this time with solid preparation.

Job or no job, remember that the wire services are a great source of information because they cover such a wide range of news. As a freelancer, it's invaluable to have contacts in the bureau. To complete your initial round of meetings with all the right people, you might consult the local phone book, directory assistance, journalists at local media, or the government's offi-

cial press guide for journalists, if one exists. In Spain, this annual guide is the most convenient source for contact numbers
in the press corps.

For leads on resident freelancers, try talking to staff foreign
correspondents or the press attaché at your country's consulate
or embassy (where it's a good idea to inform authorities that
you're in-country). Another good source of information can be
the foreign correspondents' association, if there is one. Ask
every journalist you meet for names of other contacts and how
to reach them. This will save time and effort, and enable you to
mention a reference when you call to set up an appointment.

In retrospect, John Pollack's initial round of contacts in
Madrid was quite productive. At the time, however, it seemed
discouraging. Pollack started networking on a pay phone with
a fistful of strange coins, the din of traffic in the background.
He dialed the number of a former *New York Times* correspondent whose name he had gotten before leaving New York. The
woman who answered his phone quickly tired of Pollack's halt-
ing Spanish and put the correspondent on the line. Pollack explained that he was a new reporter in town, looking for advice.
Could they meet for coffee?

Late the next afternoon, a taxi dropped Pollack at the correspondent's apartment block, a modern building in a swank
neighborhood. The doorman pointed out the right door, and a
maid ushered him across gleaming marble floors to an over-
stuffed couch, surrounded by modern art and rare antiquities.
As in a museum, brilliant track lighting illuminated the finest
pieces. A black grand piano dominated the room. Pollack sat
down, heart pounding. In walked the correspondent he aspired
to be.

Pollack had scarcely introduced himself and explained his
purpose when the blunt, veteran reporter got right to the point.
"Nobody in the United States cares about Spain. There's nothing going on here. What are you going to write about?" he said.
The contempt and frustration in his voice hit Pollack like a

bucket of ice-water. Here was a former *New York Times* foreign correspondent telling him he had blundered into the wrong country completely, a professional dead end!

Pollack feigned optimism: "Well, the Olympics are coming up, and the World's Fair . . ."

The correspondent cut him off. "Just how many stories can you write on the World's Fair? One? Two?"

Pollack knew better than to argue, so he sat and listened as the harangue continued. The thought occurred to Pollack that maybe the correspondent was right, but he couldn't bear the humiliating thought of leaving Spain without filing a single story.

Changing tack, Pollack pressed the correspondent for practical information: Who else should he talk to? How could he get press credentials? Did he have any contacts in the Jewish community, because Pollack had some story ideas about modern Jews in Spain, five hundred years after the Inquisition had forced their ancestors into exile.

At the correspondent's instruction, the maid brought him a black address book, well-thumbed and stuffed with extra papers. He read off a few names and phone numbers, mostly of other correspondents, and Pollack scribbled them into a notebook. Thanking him for his time and leads, Pollack left. "What a cold fish!" Pollack wrote in his journal. But he did get some potential contacts.

One of them, a stringer for a major U.S. business magazine, agreed to meet Pollack for a quick coffee a few days later. She made the former *New York Times* man look positively cheerful. News from Spain, she said, was so slow that she had gone into the fake fireplace business. After twenty years of journalism in Madrid, she was thinking of calling it quits.

Pollack had visions of this middle-aged woman going door-to-door like Arthur Miller's Willy Loman, hawking translucent plastic logs pulsating with a dim, electric glow. How grim, he thought. A stringer for a top magazine reduced to selling fake fireplaces? Here he was in Madrid, hoping to launch his career as a foreign correspondent, and the pros were saying it couldn't be done.

Their chat didn't last long, thankfully. At the end of the conversation, she told Pollack of an international environmental journal that needed a stringer. It didn't pay much, but it might be an opportunity. He dutifully wrote down the editor's name and number and thanked her, because early goodwill is all-important. Yet the string was virtually worthless, paying a mere two cents per word. Pollack never bothered to send a single story because better opportunities soon emerged. But he never expressed anything except honest gratitude for the lead the stringer had offered, however meager.

Alan Riding of *The New York Times* urges freelancers to swallow their pride, if that's what it takes to get going. "Some newcomers say they don't want to cover trades; they want to be *New York Times* bureau chief," he said. "You must start somewhere."

ANSWERING TRICK QUESTIONS
WITHOUT SWALLOWING YOUR FOOT

During these introductory rounds, many people you meet will be sizing you up. You need their help to get started, and making a good impression is important. The unfortunate reality is that most new stringers have little credibility with their more established colleagues, who have seen a lot of wannabes come and go. In trendy destinations like Prague in the mid-nineties, there are always a certain number of ersatz freelancers hanging around the press center talking the talk but rarely selling stories. "Every big international story has its hangers-on," said Ann Marsh. "Many are bungling and inept, but some of the best writers occasionally emerge from their ranks."

When making your introductory rounds, try to anticipate the questions colleagues will ask. Brief, direct answers are best.

Don't be afraid of silence. Prepare for the following queries, which are bound to arise in one form or another.

- Why did you come here? (Are you a serious journalist or just fooling around?)

  Emphasize professional goals, without seeming too aggressive. Tell them you want to become a foreign correspondent and have come to get experience. You might add why you selected the country you did: culture, politics, or language. Tell them you like challenges.

- What is your background? (Can you cut it?)

  Give a brief overview of your professional experience. Generally, it's a good idea to say that your old job—even if boring or unsatisfactory—was a good experience but that you wanted a new challenge. Grousing about why you quit marks you as a complainer, no matter how justified your frustrations. If you are a recent college graduate without work experience, mention any relevant academic background, including language studies, and emphasize your desire to live and work abroad. It takes guts to launch a career in a foreign land, and you are attempting it. Remember, it's hard to criticize enthusiasm.

- Who do you plan to string for? (Do you have your own connections, or are you trying to steal my job?)

  Respond to this question with some variation on the following: "I'm not sure. It depends on which strings are taken. I don't want to step on anybody's turf. What's your advice?" By taking this approach, you defuse potential challenges and avoid the embarrassment of naming their string or that of a colleague. If you have lined up a string and it's fairly obscure, consider mentioning it. First, it shows that you know about trade publications (see chapter 5: Making Ends Meet). It also suggests that you've got some food on your plate, and won't be desperate to steal their job.

> ***Important Tip:*** If you think you have lined up a major string, don't mention it. Ask who has what strings to make sure nobody has it, then file a few stories to stake out your claim. You need to cultivate a relationship with editors through solid work before you can truly secure a string and defend it against turf-jumpers.

- How long are you planning to stay? (Are you worth my time?)
  Most correspondents will not invest in you personally or professionally if they think you'll be gone in a few months, or even a year. If you tell them you're not sure how long you're staying, or that you'll see how it goes, they might not take you seriously. The best answer is vague, but confident. "Well, I came on a one-way ticket and I plan to make a go of it here." Tell them that you need to find work, but that you have enough savings to tide you over. Hinting at modest financial security suggests that you are willing to make an investment of time and money. From their perspective, if you're going to be around awhile, you might be worth getting to know.

In these interviews, ask about job openings at wire services, local English-language dailies, magazines, radio stations, and TV networks. Which strings are available? What kinds of stories are selling? Who's buying? What are they paying? Which ongoing stories need to be followed closely? Who are the people to watch? Your goal is to survey the professional and cultural landscape, and look for a plot to cultivate. Be patient but persistent. If you talk with enough people, leads will turn up.

ESTABLISHING CREDIBILITY

A freelancer's credibility is everything. Without the institutional weight of a major news organization behind you, gaining timely access to sources and news sites demands an extra measure of *chutzpah* and determination. If CNN, the *Los Angeles Times*, or ABC News wants to interview a foreign official, they are usually quickly accommodated. Unfortunately, most new freelancers don't command such respect, and are sometimes subject to runarounds from sources who think freelancers are unimportant or suspect.

Recognizing this handicap, freelancers must develop a strategy to compensate. Projecting self-confidence is essential. A purposeful stride, a provocative question, and a ready smile will take you far.

The United States Information Service (USIS), which staffs the press offices at U.S. embassies around the world, has no universal policy regarding its dealings with freelance foreign correspondents. Rather, each post develops its own guidelines based on common sense and the experience that its press attaché and foreign service officers have had with freelancers around the world, said Joan McKniff, a USIS officer at the U.S. Embassy in Madrid.

"If somebody has a letter of accreditation, that goes a lot further than someone who says, 'Trust me, I'm from *The Washington Post* and I want to interview the Ambassador,' and takes up half your day," McKniff said. But a professional approach and professional appearance will also open doors, she added.

While such letters of accreditation may not be immediately forthcoming from client media, you do need to pursue proper documentation in the interim. Consider the following.

- The most useful and easiest form of documentation is one that is most easily overlooked: a business card. Presenting someone with a business card is a quick and polite means of establishing credibility. It often evokes a card in return, thereby establishing a professional relationship from the outset (and providing the spelling of a person's name and their title, address, and phone number).

  Unfortunately, printing business cards before you leave

your home country is probably not an option, unless you know the address of your new home, and its telephone number. Even then, carrying a box of business cards past customs into a foreign land can raise uncomfortable, visa-related questions you probably want to avoid. Most major cities have printers, though perhaps not many as convenient or inexpensive as those at home. Some European capitals have coin-operated machines in the subways to make business cards on the run. Plan to get cards printed as soon as you are settled with an address and telephone number.

Simple cards are best, and should include your name, title ("Journalist" is best, in the local language), address, phone, and fax. If you don't have a fax, or if it requires manual activation before reception, omit this number and deliver it orally, as necessary. Some freelancers list their strings on their business card. This is fine, provided you are not misrepresenting yourself. Nothing will anger an editor more or destroy your credibility more thoroughly than representing yourself inaccurately or deceptively. If you have a solid professional relationship with a news outlet and its editors— and that means having sold them many stories—you may consider putting that name on your card. You don't always have to ask an editor for permission, but you should carefully evaluate whether listing the string is absolutely necessary and will be helpful to your work. When in doubt, don't.

Important Tip: A business card accompanied by an American, British, or Canadian passport will open most doors, and usually forestalls requests for official press accreditation.

- The other document you should obtain is an official press pass from the government of the host country, if such a pass exists. While a press pass may rarely be necessary—depending on the country—this credential can prove invaluable in crossing police lines, gaining access to disaster areas, key government press conferences, and sporting events you may need to cover. Follow the steps for obtaining accreditation outlined in chapter 3: Getting Ready to Go.

TOWARD YOUR FIRST STORY

If the news breaks right and the contacts work out, you could—like Dan Baum in Nairobi—file a story your first day abroad. Customarily, though, filing that first story usually takes a few weeks or more.

About eleven weeks after Steve LeVine had surprised his bosses by quitting his AP job in West Virginia, a sports editor in his old Charleston bureau spotted LeVine's byline on a story from Manila, and let out a whoop of triumph. LeVine had done it!

"The ones who had looked at me askance still did," said LeVine, whose faraway friends kept him informed. "But the other staffers threw up a cheer. I had made it out."

Al Goodman had been working for about two months in the English-language service of Spain's state-run news agency when he managed to interest a *Dallas Times Herald* editor in a story on King Juan Carlos's upcoming visit to Texas.

So, on a lazy September afternoon, Goodman hailed a taxi and told the driver, in heavily accented Spanish, to go to the king's palace on the outskirts of Madrid. The cabby shot back a skeptical glance, as if to say this crazy foreigner had no chance of getting past the machine-gun-toting guards outside the palace gates. But as they pulled up to the compound, Goodman flashed a National Writers Union press credential, a guard found him listed on the appointments schedule, and the steel barrier across the road lifted.

The drive continued another few miles through forested grounds where deer and wild boar roamed freely. Shortly they reached a low stone wall, another set of guards, and then the king's palace itself. A far cry from Disney's vision of turrets, soaring battlements, and a drawbridge, this was a split-level edifice of granite and pink brick, rebuilt during the Franco era on the site of a former royal hunting lodge. The king, a man of relatively modest tastes, had chosen to live here instead of the elaborate 2,800-room Royal Palace in central Madrid.

Ushered inside to a waiting room, Goodman marveled at the elegant, classical appointments. He settled onto the plushly up-holstered couch, examined a delicate, miniature sailing ship on the table in front of him, and tried to imagine life as royalty. Then one of the king's men—his multilingual press chief—arrived and invited Goodman into the palace press office.

Throughout the interview, Goodman kept hoping the king would drop by and grant an unscheduled audience. It didn't happen, but Goodman did get the story: Spain's efforts to project a modern, dynamic image in Texas as the showcase year of 1992 approached. The story paid $150 and got Goodman thinking that he was really going to enjoy freelancing.

John Pollack's first story was for *USA Today*. The headline topped page 7B: CONVENIENCE STORES CAPTURE SPAIN. 7-ELEVEN LEADS CHARGE OF U.S.-STYLE 24-HOUR OUTLETS. The story had grown out of Pollack's difficult first days a few months earlier when 7-Eleven was his main source of sustenance. The idea developed as follows. Most neighborhood markets closed for a long siesta at midday and all day on Sundays. But 24-hour convenience stores like 7-Eleven had been opening by the dozen in Madrid, catering to young Spaniards crazy about convenience. One day, reading Fodor's guide to Spain, Pollack learned that the Moors had begun their conquest of Spain in the year 711. There was the peg: the second invasion of "7-Eleven," but this time it was a conquest of convenience! He put in a cold call to *USA Today*'s international editor, and the story was sold. Better yet, nobody in Madrid had the *USA Today* string, and Pollack had just staked a claim.

A week later, Pollack searched the six or eight major news kiosks that dot Madrid's bustling Gran Vía, each one a veritable library of newspapers, magazines, dailies from around the globe, self-help tapes, and raunchy porn videos. *USA Today's* distribution was spotty in Madrid, sometimes arriving days late. There weren't any at the first place, and none at the second or the third. One yellowing copy turned up at the fourth, but it was the wrong date. Then, at the fifth kiosk, Pollack found the issue he was looking for. Spotting the bylined story, Pollack let out a whoop that startled passersby. "It's my article! It's my article!"

The news vendor was a short Spaniard with a white mustache who seemed to take the excitement with great calm. Bursting with pride, Pollack quickly explained how he had set out to become a foreign correspondent, then jabbed at the byline. "That's ME!" Pollack said. The vendor smiled. "You have begun," he said.

Your first story can come from anywhere, so think creatively. Plunge into the culture, however difficult or intimidating. Read a local newspaper every day, even if you have to wear out the pages of your dictionary looking up every other word in the news. Talk to people in cafés and stores. Asking a question is a good way to start a conversation. Be aggressive about your networking, professionally and socially. Throwing yourself into your new surroundings will help keep you busy instead of lonely and worried. Read history and literature, and watch TV as much as possible. No matter how hard it may be, chip away at learning the local language. Consider enrolling in a language course.

This total immersion is the crash course from which story ideas grow. When your first story is published or broadcast, it will be a watershed moment in your career as a freelance foreign correspondent. It may take awhile, so be persistent. In the end, the quality of your work matters much more than the speed at which you generate your first foreign dateline.

Steve LeVine tells new freelancers not to get obsessed about churning out copy. "Editors probably aren't sitting at their desks wondering why that new guy hasn't filed yet this week. Instead, the new freelancer should focus on making sure that his or her story is a great, developed, novel topic or angle, clearly and brightly written, and with all the style, spelling, names, punctuation, and numbers right. That's what an editor is going to remember."

5 MAKING ENDS MEET

Want to earn $350 in a single day as a free-lance foreign correspondent? Here's the assignment: A fugitive Cuban-American, wanted for swindling millions of dollars in a Florida health-care scam, has been arrested in Spain and faces an extradition hearing in a Madrid court. CNN will pay you $150 to direct a camera crew covering the story for a morning, and the *Miami Herald*—which has a special interest in all things Cuban—is offering you $200 for a story on the hearing's outcome.

Al Goodman got that assignment, and it was the kind of day that reminded him how satisfying it is to freelance abroad. Inevitably, however, there are many more days of less interesting work at modest pay. By its very nature, freelancing abroad is a cyclical business with exciting periods of intense pressure and frustrating droughts of media disinterest, no matter what stories you pitch. Therefore, to make ends meet as a stringer, you must learn how to ride these ups and downs effectively. Hard work alone is not the answer. According to Alan Riding of *The New York Times*: "It pays to think of yourself as Stringer, Inc."

DEVELOPING A HEALTHY MIX OF STRINGS
· ·

The key to steady income lies in developing a variety of outlets for your work. In the parlance of the profession, you must develop a healthy mix of strings. Elements of this mix fall into two basic categories. The first are "blue-chip" strings, such as major newspapers, popular news magazines, wire services, and major radio and television networks. These prestige news outlets permit you to showcase your talent and often generate deep professional satisfaction. It feels great to see your byline in the *Los Angeles Times*, or know that the breaking news reports you file to National Public Radio will be heard by listeners across the United States. But these strings can be tough to get and usually don't provide enough income by themselves to make a living.

All too often, stringers fall into a professional trap, said Brazilian TV cameraman Adolfo Cañadas, by working long hours for demanding, big-time clients, charging too small a fee, and neglecting to generate a real income. "Freelancers are so busy working, they don't have time to make any money," he laments.

The second category of strings are the "bread-and-butter" strings. These may include a blue-chip news outlet that wants a steady flow of reports from your country. More typically, they are specialized trade publications covering decidedly unglamorous topics like trade regulation, international securities law, or electrical energy output. Dismiss these opportunities at your peril. Clayton Jones, *The Christian Science Monitor* foreign editor, calls them "the sugar-daddy clients." Writing for the monthly newsletter *World Intellectual Property Report* may not have the same cachet as doing on-camera reports for CNN, but it has helped Goodman pay the bills. It also helps build a financial cushion that permits him to undertake more difficult, sometimes less lucrative projects for major blue-chip media.

Delving into specialized topics for trade publications also gives freelancers real insights into the country in which they work, and enables them to develop informed sources who may prove helpful on other stories.

Most successful freelance foreign correspondents develop a working mix of blue-chip and bread-and-butter strings. When news is hot, they concentrate on their major media. When things are quieter, they focus on their bread-and-butter strings: the newsletters, the monthlies, the reports. Editors at these smaller publications can be accommodating about their needs if you suddenly are pressed into covering breaking news; they may even appreciate the fact that you also work for CNN or the *Los Angeles Times*, because it means you're good at what you do.

American Amy Waldman became an agile juggler of media clients in South Africa in the run-up to 1994's historic presidential elections, in which Nelson Mandela was elected South Africa's first black president. Her healthy portfolio of strings included the *Houston Chronicle, The Christian Science Monitor, Village Voice*, and *L.A. Weekly*.

She also reported for lesser-known media such as the *Southern African Economist*, a Zimbabwe periodical that paid her $300 for three stories per month; in addition, there was the Women's Feature Service in New Delhi, India, that paid $100 for each story about women and development issues. "It was a question of writing a lot to pay my bills," Waldman said.

In Venezuela, Edward Holland quit his job as a local hire at Reuters in 1989 because he was getting paid only in the local currency—the Bolivar—and he thought he could make more money freelancing. He was right, soon boosting his income up to $2,000 a month. For the next three years, his mix of strings included *Time* magazine, which paid him $100 day rates, the *Miami Herald*, Knight-Ridder Financial News, the Fairchild newsletter *Metals Week*, and some Venezuelan economic journals published in English. "I made better money because I was earning in dollars," Holland recalled, noting too that his freelancing gambit coincided with a coup, student riots, and important economic news that caught the attention of American editors.

A balance of strings like Waldman's or Holland's will work well as long as your media do not compete with each other directly. *The Times* of London, for example, would be dismayed to learn that one of its stringers was covering the same stories for *The Guardian*. Blue-chip media keep a close watch on their stringers, so the best way to avoid conflicts is to be honest. Inform your editors and producers about your other clients. If they perceive any conflicts, you can then make an informed choice about whom you want to work for, rather than letting a surprised and angry editor make that decision for you.

Some freelancers occasionally write under multiple pen names for competing publications, and others have been known to report for rival broadcasters by disguising their voices with a handkerchief over a phone's mouthpiece. But take this advice: Your integrity and reputation are not worth sacrificing for a few extra dollars. Your byword should be candor when dealing with editors, and you'll avoid sticky situations later.

SELLING THE SAME STORY
MORE THAN ONCE

While avoiding conflicts is essential, so is developing complementary strings. Selling slightly different versions of the same story to different media is a time-honored tradition among freelancers, whether at home or abroad. For example, Al Goodman covers Spanish wines for the bi-monthly *Wine Spectator*, a magazine for wine connoisseurs. Repackaging much of the same, specialized material for a broader audience, he can readily write wine/travel features for general interest publications such as the *International Herald Tribune*.

Similarly, Goodman reported on the alleged Miami swindler's extradition hearing for both CNN and the *Miami Herald*, reporting once and filing twice. The key was that they were noncompeting media.

In another example, John Pollack wrote a feature for the *Los Angeles Times* about Cristina Sánchez, Spain's leading female bullfighter. Then he sold a different version to a magazine called *Europe*, and still another version to The Associated Press. By substituting quotes, restructuring the story, and making selected cuts, Pollack parlayed a few phone interviews and an afternoon's outing to the bullring into nearly $1,000.

Many newspapers and magazines insist that all news and feature stories they publish (except for wire reports) be original material. Small journals rarely want previously published work either. More than one stringer has been canned for sending a story to an obscure journal when the piece had already appeared in another little-known business publication. Yet many editors don't mind if you rewrite and re-sell a piece to others after the original article has appeared in their publication; just be sure to ask whether they demand anything more than "first publication rights" for freelance articles. If possible, always discuss with them any potential conflicts in advance. In the case of Pollack's coverage of the woman bullfighter, there was no conflict; after selling the story to the *Los Angeles Times*, he was free to write different versions for noncompeting media—both of which knew of his other clients.

A breaking news story that requires regular updating throughout the day or over the course of several days can be an especially lucrative assignment. When Basque separatists in Madrid tried to assassinate Spain's leading conservative politician with a car bomb in 1995, Goodman started coverage with an alert to CNN. As it often does in major attacks of this kind, CNN requested a "beeper"—a live phone interview—with the anchor desk. That paid $50. Then he pitched the story to CBC national radio in Canada, which took a radio spot of one minute and 10 seconds, paying $50. Then he pitched the news to NPR, which paid $30 for a 45-second radio spot. After one cycle of news—a few hours of work—Goodman had earned $130. A major development in the story would generate a new round of reports for the three media, and Goodman would pocket another $130, for a total of $260 on the day. For these types of stories Goodman essentially does the reporting once, but he packages it for different media and sells it several times.

Nick Anderson, freelancing from Mexico City, did the same thing when he decided that a four-day-old peasant protest in the Mexican state of Tabasco was turning into a hot story. Monitoring the news for a Copley News Service correspondent who was out of town, Anderson learned that thousands of angry, left-leaning peasants were blocking roads to some government-owned oil installations. They claimed that Pemex, Mexico's state-run oil company, had polluted their land and water but refused to pay compensation. Police and military units cleared the roads, but after security forces withdrew, the protesters quickly gathered again.

"I wrote that story based on television and radio reports in the capital, and filed to Copley. But it seemed like the story was getting warmer, not cooler, so I thought it might make a good one-day road trip."

Anderson persuaded the returning Copley correspondent, who was too busy to leave town again, to pay him $200 for a news feature from Tabasco. And expenses? Copley would pay only "a few dollars" for local taxis and telephone calls, which was a problem because the round-trip airfare was $170. "It wouldn't make much sense for me economically to work my ass off for a net gain of $30," Anderson remembers. "So I tried to find another outlet for the story."

He called the Mexico City bureau of *The Christian Science Monitor*, where he occasionally pinch-hit. The correspondent, Howard LaFranchi, also was too busy to go to Tabasco and didn't have a freelance budget. But he urged Anderson to pitch the story directly to the *Monitor*'s newsroom in Boston. Just don't emphasize the story's political angle, LaFranchi advised Anderson, because the *Monitor* had just run a piece on the peasants' leftist political party.

By pitching *Monitor* editors a story on major peasant clashes with Mexican police near the oil fields, Anderson lined up a 700-word assignment that paid $175 and no expenses. For good measure, Anderson called the *Newsweek* correspondent, who politely declined. "At least he knew I was on the ball and following the news," Anderson said.

Having lined up $375 in income for a story that would cost about $170 in expenses, Anderson was in business. A staff colleague covering the story for Knight-Ridder even agreed to let him share her taxi at no cost. "I had achieved my economic goal. I wanted the story to be a quick, one-day trip that would net $200," he said.

As it happened, Anderson picked the right day to go, witnessing the most violent clash yet between police and the peasants. He filed two stories, each tailored with a distinct angle for his clients, and was back in Mexico City twelve hours after he had left. To ice the cake, *Newsweek* called him a few days later to work on a different story.

TAILORING YOUR STORY PITCHES
TO DIFFERENT MEDIA

Howard LaFranchi's advice to Anderson to downplay the peasants' political affiliation in his story pitch to *Monitor* editors raises an important issue. More than one freelancer has been frustrated by a newsroom's indifference to a "great" story, failing to recognize that the problem lay not with the editor or producer—or with the story—but with the way in which the stringer presented it.

How you pitch story ideas to editors and producers will always vary, but there are some common denominators to every successful pitch. First, they must be brief. You should be able to lay out the story and why it's important in just a few sentences. The main questions editors want answered are: What's the story? and Why should they care? Most readers, viewers, and listeners will skim or tune out news that doesn't seem relevant, interesting, amusing, or compelling. Editors and producers keep this in mind when considering what to publish or broadcast. You should too when you pitch them story ideas.

Pitching Breaking News
If a story is breaking and you think you can sell it, get the basic facts and quickly develop a coherent, concise pitch. Then call your media. On a breaking news story like the Madrid car bomb, Goodman made what was essentially the same pitch to CNN, NPR, and CBC. It went something like this with CNN:

OPERATOR:	Will you accept a collect call from Al Goodman in Spain?
CNN PRODUCER:	Yes. Hi, Al, we've just seen the flashes on the wires. Who is this guy who almost got killed?
GOODMAN:	He's the leader of the main opposition conservative party and most polls predict he'll be Spain's next prime minister.
PRODUCER:	How badly was he hurt?
GOODMAN:	Eyewitnesses are telling radio here that he walked away, almost miraculously, with hardly a scratch, but his armor-plated car was destroyed.
PRODUCER:	Who's behind the bomb?
GOODMAN:	No group has claimed responsibility but police say it looks like the Basque separatist group ETA. If so, it's a very bold attack for them.

PRODUCER:	We'll use you for a sixty-second beeper next hour.
GOODMAN:	Will the anchor ask questions?
PRODUCER:	Probably one, after your intro. We'll call you back in forty minutes, five minutes before the hour. Find out everything you can till then. Bye.

The elapsed time for this conversation was about thirty-five seconds. The producer asked just a few questions and wanted concise answers in order to figure out whether the story was worth using, and, if so, in what manner. Note that he already trusted Goodman, who had established his credibility through many previous stories.

Pitching Features
It usually takes longer to secure an assignment when pitching features, but remember that most editors and producers still like to have the story summary in a sentence or two. If a story is extremely visual, be sure to mention the potential for great photography. Feature proposals are usually best submitted in a memo via e-mail or fax.

For example, Goodman faxed CNN a pitch on a fiesta in northwest Spain in which ranchers herd wild horses into corrals to trim their manes and tails for summer. The first sentence of the pitch was: "You know it's summertime in Spain when the wild horses come down from the hills to get a haircut." And to give the story some teeth, Goodman also mentioned that this fiesta stood in sharp contrast to the widely held stereotype that Spaniards mistreat animals, as many people feel they do in bullfights. In truth, bullfights are not uniformly popular in Spain, and many people in the northwest prefer the fiesta of the wild horses.

CNN bit, and Goodman got the story.

GETTING THE MOST FROM
SCHEDULED NEWS EVENTS

Big scheduled news events, like national elections, also present great opportunities to juggle work for various media. This takes careful planning. For example, when polls indicated that Spain's Socialist Prime Minister Felipe González might lose the 1993 general elections after nearly eleven years in power, the international media flocked to Madrid, sensing a historic shift back to the right in the land once ruled by dictator Francisco Franco. During the final days of the campaign, Goodman started his coverage by arranging key interviews and translating for a CBC Radio staff correspondent sent to Madrid to cover the elections. Earning $150 a day as the CBC "fixer," Goodman also carried his tape recorder to some of the interviews, which formed the basis of his own reports for NPR.

As election day approached and Goodman's commitments to NPR grew more demanding, he arranged for another freelancer to take over as the CBC fixer. Goodman then prepared coverage for NPR and an advance election report for CNN, including his first on-camera "standup." The latter paid $500.

On election day, Goodman filed "the polls are open" stories for NPR and CNN, later reported on the results, and prepared an on-camera wrap-up for CNN the next day. By week's end, he had earned $1,500. Prime Minister González, by the way, spoiled the story about "historic change in Spain" by winning his fourth consecutive term. In 1996, González lost trying for a fifth.

FINDING A NICHE

Some stringers who find a lucrative niche don't need a large variety of strings to make ends meet. Bangkok-based Daniel

Pruzin says that "the vast majority of my stories are business-related. They cover everything from trade negotiations to investment regulation to new auto and steel mill projects in the region." His bread and butter is the Bureau of National Affairs (BNA), Inc., a Washington, D.C., business publication group. Pruzin also reports for *Multichannel News*, a New York–based cable and satellite TV industry magazine; Detroit-based *Automotive Industries*; London-based *Airtrade* (on the air cargo industry); and some of the *Financial Times*'s health-care newsletters. In 1996, Pruzin estimated that he was earning upwards of $35,000 annually.

PHOTOGRAPHY AND TELEVISION FOOTAGE

Freelance photography—a subject with its own "how-to" books—should not be ignored by journalists focusing on print journalism. Good pictures help sell stories, and when pitching ideas to editors it's useful to emphasize that you've got terrific "art" to go with the story. Modern camera technology allows even amateur photographers to shoot pictures good enough for publication—the trick is choosing the right shots and taking enough of them. Various publications pay $50–$100 for each photo that accompanies a story, so why not shoot an entire roll of film while you're reporting the story? Even mug shots of the people you interview are worth the investment. If a $200–$300 camera seems expensive, consider that the sale of just a few photos will pay for it.

It's worth remembering, though, that when big news is breaking, major publications almost always rely on the wire services for photos. Freelancers who try to compete with the wires on breaking news usually end up frustrated. It's better for stringers to focus on feature photography to accompany their written work.

In most cases, sending negatives or color slides to an editor by express mail or international courier service (UPS, Federal Express, or DHL) is fast enough for freelance purposes. However, technology enabling you to transmit photos electronically is both improving and dropping in price. If a news outlet is in a big hurry to receive a photo you've shot, they will typically direct you to the nearest bureau of the Associated Press, Reuters, or Agence France Presse to send an urgent "special to" photo through the bureau's state-of-the-art equipment.

Television is another outlet for pictures. Like the roving freelance photographers who shoot international news, there is a parallel corps of roving freelance TV camera operators. One of them is Gibraltar native Henry Bautista, who for two decades has traveled the world as a freelance cameraman for ABC and CBS. Bautista typically goes to hot spots on temporary assignment— for days, weeks, or even months—with the full backing and support of a major network. "As a freelance cameraman, it's much better to be assigned by a network or news agency," he said.

A typical two-person camera crew (camera operator and sound technician with all necessary gear) on assignment for a major network may earn $1,100 to $1,400 per day. Jobs lasting more than a week can be negotiated. The network pays all of the crew's expenses while it's on assignment, including lodging and communications, and provides a per diem. Insist on insurance if you're going on a dangerous assignment.

Most international news crews contract themselves at a full-day rate only, because accepting half-day assignments might preclude tackling more lucrative full-day assignments from other clients. Some crews prefer to rent gear but many professionals, like Bautista, own their own equipment because it's more reliable. A typical crew travels with ten to fourteen cases of equipment worth $60,000 to $180,000, including the camera, lenses, tripod, lights, audio mixers, microphones, playback deck, playback adapter, monitor, accessory cables, batteries, and battery chargers.

To make ends meet, Bautista works out of three home bases:

London, Johannesburg, and Saddle Brook, New Jersey—the latter for its quick access to airports and clients across the river in New York City.

Madrid-based Michael Moffett takes a different approach to television freelancing, alternating assignments as a correspondent, producer, and cameraman. He earns a bit more than half of his income as a correspondent and producer for a 30-minute weekly program called *European Journal*. Produced in English by the German broadcaster Deutsche Welle TV, the program is shown on PBS affiliates in the United States, on Canadian TV, and in Asia. Moffett produces two or three reports each month—about 10 minutes of material—which include his on-camera stand-ups as correspondent. He negotiates a single fee per report from Deutsche Welle TV, and from that sum he hires a two-person camera crew ($325 to $645 per day) to shoot the footage in Betacam video format, hires an editor and tape-editing facilities ($120 for each minute of finished, broadcast-ready report), and then pays himself.

Moffett also works as a cameraman in a newer format of television news which uses a smaller, Hi-8 camera. For these reports, which include everything except a correspondent's stand-up, he is a "one-man band," serving as cameraman and producer. His client is Video News International, a *New York Times*–owned company based in Philadelphia. Video News International typically commissions feature stories with broad international appeal, running from 4 to 10 minutes. The company can then send footage and a suggested script to TV clients in countries such as Japan, Brazil, Taiwan, Great Britain, or France, where native announcers voice-over the script in the local language. Conveniently, each client can use the material in its entirety or in a shortened version, much the same way that a newspaper can run full or abbreviated wire stories. Video News International trained Moffett during a one-month course and supplied him with the $3,000 camera, a tripod, batteries, tapes, and a viewing monitor. Moffett typically files one report per month, about five minutes of television news, and that accounts for just under half of his monthly income.

Still a third model for overseas television is Al Goodman's job as CNN's freelance correspondent in Spain. Goodman does not work as a cameraman at all, but instead as a correspondent and producer. Like Moffett for Deutsche Welle TV, Goodman receives a set fee from CNN, typically at least $1,000 for each completed, two-minute report. That fee covers Goodman's pay, the cost of the camera crew, the cost of shipping the tape by air cargo to London or Atlanta, and other expenses. Goodman often lowers expenses by sending a shortened "rough-cut" version of his report directly to CNN, where it will undergo the final edit in a CNN edit booth. Goodman can earn $300 or more per package.

BUILDING PROFESSIONAL RELATIONSHIPS

Phone calls to editors out of the blue—unavoidable in freelancing—can and do kick off successful professional relationships. But they tend to be hit-or-miss, often depending on the editor's mood or the relative degree of chaos in the newsroom when the call comes in. Therefore, freelancers who never establish steady relationships with editors are doomed to frenetic and short-lived stints as foreign correspondents, because each story pitch means "cold calling" a different client. Your challenge is to develop steady, professional relationships so that when you call, the editor can focus on your story ideas and not on your background or ability to complete the job.

Once you have established yourself with a particular news outlet, editors there will treat you much like a staffer—minus the expense account. Editors who know and like your work will be more inclined to accept unusual or off-beat stories that would be hard to sell on a cold call. John Pollack sold the *Los Angeles Times* a $500 story on the importance of the pig in

Spanish culture. That's right, the Spanish pig, for centuries an animal of remarkable political, religious, and social significance on the Iberian Peninsula. The story probably would have been impossible to sell on a first-time call, but Pollack already had a good working relationship with the paper's correspondent for southern Europe, who was looking for features from Spain.

In another instance, Pollack sold Chicago-based *Advertising Age* a brief story on Spanish underwear. It was a cinch, because the man pitching the shorts on Spanish television was Michael Jordan, the basketball superstar, his voice dubbed into flawless Spanish. Jordan's endorsement fee was worth probably six figures. *Ad Age* paid Pollack—its regular Spain stringer—75 bucks. Again, the established relationship was essential to selling the story.

If at first you have difficulty developing strings, don't get discouraged. Turnover is fairly common among freelance foreign correspondents, and good strings often open up unexpectedly. Usually, editors ask departing freelancers to identify potential replacements; if you are well respected in the local freelance community, a colleague might recommend you. This is called "trading up": taking on a more prestigious or better-paying client, and passing off a less desirable string to another freelancer. Naturally, enterprising freelancers can also make a lot of progress on their own, without waiting to inherit strings.

Amy Waldman got a good break in South Africa after meeting Bill Keller, then a *New York Times* foreign correspondent, at a Nelson Mandela campaign rally in 1994. She asked Keller for work. He asked to see her clips. Nothing happened right away, but she kept crossing paths with him at other news events. As the election grew closer, Keller hired her for $150 per day to assist with research. Waldman also got to suggest stories, and scored her first byline in the *Times* on election day. It was a piece on how blacks and whites on South Africa's death row perceived the historic election.

Persistence, luck, and creativity are three ingredients for securing strings and story assignments. So is your ability to develop good contacts. Al Goodman used a combination of these elements to build and broaden his portfolio of strings over several years in Madrid.

Goodman's first steady strings in Spain had a lot to do with good contacts. A friend from a paper in California had become an editor for the *Wine Spectator* and needed a stringer in Spain; at National Public Radio, Goodman knew editors through their mutual work in the National Writers Union; and at the *International Herald Tribune*, a friend and former UPI bureau chief in Madrid opened the door.

Goodman also made his own breaks, responding to a classified ad in the *International Herald Tribune* seeking a Madrid correspondent for the Bureau of National Affairs. Soon, Goodman was covering Spain for a variety of BNA business newsletters. Next came the Canadian Broadcasting Corporation radio string, a job Goodman landed after he happened to sit next to CBC's London correspondent at a Margaret Thatcher news conference in Madrid.

Later, CNN called the U.S. Embassy press office in Madrid for freelance contacts who might be available to help cover Spain's banner year of 1992. Goodman was on the list, and so was his friend Ben Jones, an American on staff at EFE, Spain's state-run international news agency. CNN liked Jones because of his journalistic credentials and his access to breaking news through EFE. But EFE, worried about getting short-changed, threatened to put Jones on the graveyard shift if he accepted the CNN string. Jones, a new father at the time, opted to keep his day job. Then CNN gave Goodman a chance.

However you hook up with potential clients—through colleagues or cold calls—you will quickly have to deliver the goods. At many media, a stringer's most precarious moments are in the beginning, a trial period in which editors determine if your work is good enough. They may decide to dump you, or they may offer help, encouragement, and guidance. If they're satisfied, better assignments will start coming your way before long.

For CNN, Goodman started with an occasional voice-over of video footage, and the work later grew to include phone interviews with the anchor desk—live question-and-answer sessions with an anchor back in the studio—and on-camera reporting.

Eventually, Goodman became so adept at picking up strings that he ran into a problem: too many masters. At one point, he was trying to keep ten clients satisfied on a regular basis, including *Business Week*, the *Miami Herald*, *The Christian Science Monitor*, CNN, CBC, and *Condé Nast Traveler* magazine. His business card said "journalist" and listed six clients, prompting wry Spaniards to remark that Goodman "had clearly entered the age of multimedia." It was too much. So he scaled back. After securing *The New York Times* string, which paid a $600 monthly retainer, he dropped *Business Week*, the *Miami Herald*, *The Christian Science Monitor*, and CBC, suggesting other freelance colleagues for the jobs.

Through the years, the number and complementary diversity of Goodman's strings have provided plenty of challenging work and enabled him to weather the ups and downs of the news market, especially the American media's on-again, off-again interest in Spain. He even survived when a *Condé Nast Traveler* on-line service, which was paying him up to $1,250 a month for eight travel briefs of 300 words each, abruptly closed.

Each stringer has to decide when enough is enough in terms of clients. Goodman found that by trimming his list of strings, he could devote more time to each regular client, do more interesting work, and make just as much money.

NEGOTIATING FEES AHEAD OF TIME

Unfortunately, all the horror stories are true about media clients "forgetting" to pay their freelancers, sending paychecks months late, and holding stories until they grow stale and then refusing freelancers their rightful kill fee. These are the perils of freelancing, and though they may sound like distant worries now, struggling to get paid can become a seemingly endless nightmare when you are the victim. Yet there are ways to avoid these pitfalls and ensure that you make ends meet.

The first is to recognize that most editors are sincere about trying to pay on time, even if the pay is low. Only a minority try to take advantage of freelancers by accepting stories they never intend to pay for. If you hear that a particular news outlet has a reputation for stiffing freelancers, refuse to work for them unless they pay in advance or you like doing charity work. If you do get burned, make sure it's only once. Never work for that organization again, and warn other freelancers about your experience.

You can avoid most payment problems if you settle the following issues before you start an assignment: how much and when you will be paid, in what currency, and what story-related expenses are reimbursable? Find out if you need to send a bill and the logistics of doing so. Is there a person in the accounting department who will be your key contact for getting paid? What is his or her name and direct phone number or extension?

As long as you remain friendly, polite, and concise, editors should not mind discussing these matters. Yours is a professional relationship. House painters, lawyers, movie actors, business consultants, and the like typically negotiate their fees and conditions in advance. Freelancing from abroad is no different.

Many media are notoriously tightfisted when dealing with freelancers. When negotiating a fee, stick up for yourself and don't be intimidated.

Most media will tell you that they pay a standard rate per story. They probably do, but they might pay more if they like your work or want the story badly enough. As a freelancer, you need to evaluate how much time and effort a particular assignment will require. Will the fee offered make it worth your while? This will vary, depending on your country's cost of living and the other opportunities you might be giving up to take the assignment. If you are broke and idle, the opportunity cost of almost any job is nil. If you are extremely busy, your time is worth more.

Instead of story rates, some media pay by the hour or by the day. Nick Anderson has been paid $10 per hour from *National Geographic* and up to $175 per day from major news magazines. Inevitably, your pay as a stringer will fluctuate, depending on the news market and your clients. When evaluating a day rate, try to calculate your pay on an hourly basis; it may help put a potential job into perspective. A day rate of $150 for an assignment may sound good, but is it worth it if it keeps you occupied from dawn until midnight? As an hourly rate, it might not seem so attractive.

Some media simply prefer paying by the hour. Typically, these are highly specialized publications. The advantage of an hourly rate is the protection it affords stringers in cases when research for a story becomes extremely time-consuming or if you cannot line up interviews immediately. And a good hourly rate can generate income quickly and efficiently on stories that go smoothly. BNA pays Goodman $25 per hour to cover stories on the environment and other business topics in Spain. A story Goodman writes for BNA might be 800 words long, but if it requires only six hours to research and write—i.e., less than a day—Goodman still earns $150, a sum greater than some other specialized media would pay for a story of that length.

But the hourly rate is not offered carte blanche. BNA has correspondents in forty-three nations and is well aware of the potential for freelance graft. Consequently, if it took twelve hours to do a 400-word story that has just one interview, BNA editors would ask you why. But BNA does recognize that not all government and business sources around the world have a tradition of talking to the press on a regular basis, as is the case in the United States. Even in countries where there is a vigorous free press, reporters for specialized publications may find access to busy officials more difficult. While many sources jump at the chance to appear on CNN, far fewer people know that BNA's *International Environment Reporter* (*INER*) does an important job of keeping its readers abreast of legislative developments around the world. Consequently, it usually takes a lot more work to get an interview with a senior government official for *INER* than it does getting one for CNN. In these cases, an hourly rate is a valuable insurance policy for the freelancer.

INTANGIBLE JOB BENEFITS

When considering whether the proposed rate is fair, try to evaluate potential hidden benefits of the job. Is it a blue-chip publication from which a clip would help land other jobs? Is it a prestige string, such as NPR, that pays relatively little but offers the professional satisfaction of doing quality, in-depth work? Do you want to get your foot in the door with a particular news organization, or with a certain editor or producer? Is the assignment too good of a journalistic opportunity to ignore? There are a lot of issues that come into play here, and sometimes taking a financial hit on a story pays greater personal and professional dividends in the long run.

EXPENSE ACCOUNTS

Editors sometimes propose low fees to freelancers because they believe stringers will pad expense accounts. Indeed, some freelancers do. But stringers who must make ends meet by padding expense accounts should consider another line of work. Avoid the temptation by negotiating a reasonable fee for each job. If the editor flatly refuses to pay a decent wage and you really want the job, then be sure to work efficiently, giving the editor just his money's worth.

After you have established a good working relationship with a client, ask its editors to pay in advance for major story expenses, such as travel and lodging. Editors often can bill these big-ticket items to a corporate credit card or have the expense money advanced to your bank account. Your goal is to avoid paying hefty expenses up front and then waiting to be repaid. If you front the cash, you are essentially loaning money to media to help them operate.

> ***Important Tip:*** Pay close attention to the exchange rate in the country where you're working versus the currency in which you will be paid. If the exchange rate fluctuates, and many do, make sure that you are reimbursed at a fair rate.

Phone companies in much of the world still do not itemize phone bills. This puts the onus on the freelancer to keep track of individual calls, because many media may be skeptical of receiving a bill for $90 in phone calls without supporting documentation. If your client insists on an itemized list of phone calls, preparing one will be a tedious task. You can make it easier by keeping track of calls as you go along. Goodman, for example, keeps a handwritten log of his telephone calls on a master list, jotting down the client and purpose of the call. When it comes time to bill calls to CNN or *The New York Times*, it's easy to find the pertinent calls and assign their costs by client and story, because he already has a list of what the calls cost by minute, based on their destination and the time the call was made.

To satisfy his clients' accountants, Goodman sends the

phone company's itemized list, if possible. Or he types a list of the calls and includes with his invoice a photocopy of the calling rate cards from AT&T or Spain's equivalent, Telefónica. He converts the amount due from pesetas into dollars at the official exchange rate. This entire bookkeeping process may take 30 minutes.

Be sure to factor in the cost of the time you spend on administrative work associated with a story when negotiating your assignment fee (see appendixes 3 and 4). Editors rarely question the expense statements of freelancers who work efficiently on the phone, do not run up unnecessary bills, and generate good stories.

GETTING PAID

Getting paid in full and on time is largely a function of careful bookkeeping, timely billing, and rapid follow-up if there is a delay in payment. To avoid delayed payments, always send the invoice as soon as the client has received the work and all editing is complete (if the story is not yet edited, editors might require you to do more reporting and incur higher expenses). Keep copies of the invoices and the receipts. Keep a separate file for each client so the records are easily accessible.

Professional invoices are easily generated on your laptop, even without the specialized software that is readily available. Each should have a number, such as 001 (1997), the name of the editor, the client name, the date of the invoice, the date the work was performed, the location where the work was performed, and a description of the work (e.g., "800-word story about the Tate Gallery," or "field-produce a CNN live satellite interview between Madrid and London with U.S. Treasury Secretary Lloyd Bentsen"). List the total amount due, and then break it down into amounts owed for the work itself and for expenses. Itemize expenses (taxi, phone, etc.) and include receipts whenever possible (see appendix 4). Write your name and the story assignment on each receipt so the accounting department to which you send it can keep track easily.

> ***Important Tip:*** Keep a single computer file with a running list of every job you've completed for every media outlet. As soon as you file a story, make a short entry in this master "jobs" file, noting the client, the date you sent the work, a slug-line for the job, and the amount due. When you are paid, make a note of that, too.

Some media pay more quickly than others, sometimes within days. Some provide their own invoice form to freelancers. Others take several months to pay, and if the absentminded editor forgets to "okay" the invoice and forward it quickly to the accounting department, payment can take what seems like an eternity. Consult your master jobs file or your separate invoice files regularly to make sure checks have been paid for each invoice, and paid in the full amount. If not, contact the editor to inquire about the delay.

Becoming a member of the National Writers Union in the United States or joining a similar organization elsewhere can help you get paid, especially on one-time jobs for media where you have less leverage than with your steady clients. Goodman once wrote a story for International Media Partners of New York, the publishers of financial periodicals. IMP faxed Goodman a signed statement promising $300 within 45 days of publication, but four months and many collect phone calls later the check for $300 still had not arrived. Goodman dashed off a letter politely informing IMP that he would soon feel obliged to contact the National Writers Union, which has won more than $1 million in back pay for writers on similar grievance issues. The check arrived promptly.

> ***Important Tip.*** While you may decide to cover stories
> for certain reputable media based on a verbal agreement,
> you should get a written contract for many other jobs,
> such as one-time articles or major assignments that could
> tie you up for days or weeks. Have the editor who hired
> you sign it (and send it by fax or mail) before beginning
> any work. The contract should include a brief description
> of the work, the deadline, your fee, expense limit, and the
> method and timing of payment, including a full or partial
> kill fee if the story is accepted but not published.

Working from Nairobi, Kenya, Patricia Reber said getting
media clients to pay up can be extremely frustrating. "I've simply dropped clients whom I have to harass about paying me."

PAYING TAXES

Just like other professionals, freelance foreign correspondents
should file tax returns in their home country and, if required,
in the country where they work. It's the law, it's the right thing
to do, and it will free you from haunting, unpaid tax bills upon
your return home.

Caitlin Randall learned the hard way. She freelanced for four
years from Peru and Costa Rica, filing regularly to the *Miami
Herald, Newsday, The Christian Science Monitor*, and Crane
Communications (including *Advertising Age*)—but not filing
anything to Uncle Sam. "I didn't file because I knew I wasn't
making enough to pay taxes," she said. Later she returned to
the United States and got a staff job at AP–Dow Jones financial
news service in New York. One day a letter arrived from the Internal Revenue Service, summoning her to a tax audit. "I had
to go through every freelance story and figure out what every
one had paid me. I had to come up with something." In the
end, the IRS estimated she owed $1,000 in back taxes. "A thou-

sand dollars may not sound like a lot of money, but I also had to take a day off from work and use an accountant to sort it all out," Randall said. "My father warned me, 'You have to file even if you don't have to pay.' He was right."

The United States has bilateral tax treaties with many foreign countries, agreements that essentially establish that workers will not be taxed twice—once by each country on the same income. U.S. tax codes also include a rule called the Foreign Income Exclusion, allowing American citizens working abroad full-time (and busy foreign freelancers can qualify for this designation) to avoid paying U.S. income tax unless they earn more than $70,000. The exclusion does not excuse Americans working abroad from filing returns, even those working illegally without the proper visa. Depending on their circumstances, American freelancers may still be liable for self-employment and social security taxes. Tax advice is available at embassies around the world, along with the necessary forms. Consulting government tax specialists is strongly recommended. Think of it this way: Your taxes are paying their salaries, so take advantage of their expertise and avoid headaches later.

Another option is hiring a tax adviser in your home country or in the country where you are working. This may be unnecessary, if your financial situation is relatively uncomplicated and you are patient about filling out tax forms. But it may be worthwhile to hire an expert if you are swamped with work, and can make more money doing your job than preparing your tax forms.

NONJOURNALISM WORK

Freelance foreign correspondents should stick to journalism. Sometimes, however, economic necessity demands that they generate income from other sources. Stephen Hess of the Brookings Institution reported in his book that 40 percent of foreign freelancers sought work other than journalism to supplement their income.

In most cases, getting started abroad may require income from savings or other sources, at least temporarily. "You've got to land with something in your pocket," said Alan Riding of *The New York Times*. If you must seek other work, try to find something complementary to journalism. One common avenue is writing advertising supplements that appear in various publications around the world. This type of work requires reporting, organizational, and writing skills but the end product will be advertising. The advertiser, or editors in their lieu, will insist on a positive spin. It can be lucrative—*Newsweek* pays $1 per word—but it may prevent you from writing about that same subject for a valued media client.

The New York Times travel editor Nancy Newhouse once had to scramble against deadline to replace a major Sunday travel story about a freelancer's cruise on an Asian river. The problem? A sharp-eyed *Times* correspondent had just spotted a similar story about the same cruise—by the same freelancer—in a *Time* magazine "advertorial." The freelancer hadn't informed the *Times* about the "advertorial." The *Times* killed his Sunday feature.

Some freelancers try to avoid using their bylines on these advertising supplements to keep their independent reputation intact, but they still run risks because editors tend to talk among themselves about who wrote what. Information about these periodic supplements is sometimes available from advertising representatives at major publications, which usually farm them out to companies that in turn hire freelancers.

The advertising supplements should be distinguished from the so-called special reports routinely published by the *International Herald Tribune, Financial Times*, or *The Wall Street Journal*. Special reports—sometimes a few pages long and sometimes an entire section—consist of in-depth news features or cultural reports about a particular region or city, stories that are assigned and edited by the newspaper's editorial staff. These stories are quality journalism and may be critical in tone. Although special reports are essentially just vehicles to attract extra advertising from a particular area or industry, advertisers don't get to see news copy before publication; the advertising and editorial staffs are separate and independent. Often, editors hire freelancers to report and write many or all of the stories. Writing special reports—unlike working on advertising supplements—can enhance your journalistic credentials and may provide solid clips.

Written translations are also an employment option. English is the dominant international language of diplomacy and commerce, and more and more companies publish documents and reports in two languages. Depending on your foreign language skills, you may be able to land lucrative translation contracts. These can be tedious, but they carry the benefit of education; you can expand your foreign vocabulary and gain a greater feeling for the language. However, you may be competing against a field of professional translators in your country. The same is true if you were to teach English as a second language. Inevitably, professional English teachers will command the best jobs and pay in this field.

One possibility for broadcast freelancers is studio dubbing. Goodman has dubbed several Spanish movies and a few cartoons into English; once he played the role of a hapless "good ol' boy" killed by a hitchhiker. All of these options should be seen as temporary remedies during periods of journalistic drought. But don't grow complacent. Keep in mind what you set out to do—become a foreign correspondent—and push hard for opportunities in this arena. Remember that news never ends, so there is always another opportunity just around the corner.

CUTTING OVERHEAD
. . . .

As noted in chapter 2, making a living as a foreign correspondent depends not just on your ability to find stories and market them successfully but on what it costs you to live and conduct business as well. Most successful freelancers have learned how to keep a low overhead, although Laura Ballman in the Ukraine may have tried too hard. While freelancing in 1995 for CBS radio and UPI, she rented a one-bedroom apartment in Kiev for $200 per month. In its day, this apartment had been a pretty decent place, home to an administrator for Aeroflot airlines. But not anymore. "One morning I was in the kitchen and heard a big crash," Ballman remembered. She ran to the living room, only to see massive chunks of plaster falling down from the ceiling. Ballman may have been making ends meet, but she still couldn't keep a roof over her head.

Cutting overhead doesn't mean living like a pauper. Simply look out for small techniques that save big money, like calling clients collect. Except for initial cold calls to editors who have no clue as to your identity or your reason for calling, you should call media clients collect. News organizations sometimes assign foreign editors a budget for freelance correspondents but do not charge collect calls from abroad to these editors' budgets. Consequently, it may cost editors nothing to find out what you have to tell them, and they may not want to miss something that could turn out to be a good story.

That said, don't waste their time. Be concise. You should be able to identify yourself and pitch your story in less than a minute, offering to discuss your professional qualifications if they're interested. If they want to chat, let them take the initiative. If they are too busy to talk, ascertain a good time to call back. Above all else, be confident: you are offering them a valuable service.

When calling collect, the worst that can happen is that somebody refuses to accept the charges. Usually this happens because the foreign editor is away from the desk or because a newsroom staffer is unfamiliar with your name. Don't take it personally.

Be extremely friendly with everyone, including the operator—they have quite a bit of latitude. When using the international services of AT&T, MCI, Sprint, British Telecom, or Bell Canada, you may be permitted to ask the party on the other end basic information, such as when your editor will return to the desk. Sometimes you can even leave a number for the editor to call you back.

If a newsroom refuses your collect call, consider waiting a few minutes and dialing again. Sometimes they change their minds on the second try, thinking it must be something urgent or serious. E-mail communication is another efficient way to reduce costs. "It's very reliable, much cheaper for the company, and much cheaper for the freelancer who's only making a local call. It makes a big difference," said Jan Jaben of *Advertising Age*. Faxes are another possibility, although they are fast becoming outmoded by paperless communications. "I hate the fax. It seems like a dinosaur," confessed Elisa Tinsley of *USA Today*.

Written story proposals allow an editor to consider a pitch in a calm moment, instead of being caught unawares during a collect phone call amidst the hubbub of the day. As soon as you've established a steady relationship with a client, try to pitch story ideas and file copy just like their staff foreign correspondents do, which often means sending written material directly into the media's computer system via modem. Ask the news outlet's computer guru to talk you through the process once, just for practice.

Editors also appreciate freelancers who hold down costs by staying with friends while they're on the road, or by patronizing modestly priced hotels. The big-time staff correspondents may travel in luxury, sipping premium brandy at $35 a glass on their newspaper's expense account, but freelancers are expected to rough it. Work out your expense budget with editors in advance, then stick to it. If not, you may well end up paying the balance out of your own pocket.

Finding a good travel agent in your foreign country can help to sharply reduce the cost of travel within the country because of access to executive discount programs on travel and lodging. Hotel coupon books are available in some countries through travel agencies or large department stores, which allow travelers to stay in fancy hotels at a third to half of the normal price. A travel agency may also save you time in crunch situations.

Freelance correspondents may be granted the occasional expense budget that allows them to enjoy the finer pleasures, but this is rare. Even when helping CNN cover the 1992 Summer Olympics in Barcelona, Goodman stayed with friends for three weeks.

If you plan ahead, road trips sometimes present the opportunity to do complementary work for different strings. If so, you might ask these media to share expenses, such as lodging, transportation, or the rental of a portable telephone. Perhaps two interested departments within the same company will underwrite the expenses. Be creative; it never hurts to ask.

For the Cable News Network's coverage of the 1995 royal wedding in Spain, CNN's International desk paid half of the costs and CNN's Spanish-language broadcast department paid the other half. That allowed Goodman, as the English-language correspondent, and Guillermo Sánchez, as the Spanish-language correspondent, to hire a camera crew, rent video-editing facilities, and travel from Madrid to Seville to cover a story that neither of their departments might have paid for individually.

Some stringers approach cost-cutting as a sport. Others elevate it to an art form. One of the finest examples involved two British stringers from prestigious, competing London dailies who flew to Madrid in 1991 to cover international negotiations on the Antarctic Treaty. True professionals, they filed to British clients during the day and to Australian papers and wires at night, a round-the-clock marathon to make their trip to Spain pay off.

Their expense budget was so tight that they decided to stay in a cheap hostel, sharing not only the same room but the same, sagging bed. As rival freelance colleagues, not lovers, they gave new meaning to the concept of making ends meet. Had their respective editors known that the competing reporters were literally in bed together, all hell would have broken loose.

But that wasn't all. Their hostel was so seedy that it didn't even have a bath or shower, only a dirty sink that sputtered water the color of rusted pipes. Aiming to look professional at the negotiations, the stringers sought out the youthful, easygoing Greenpeace delegation, which was staying at a three-star hotel. Befriending Paul Bogart, the Greenpeace spokesman, the stringers finagled much-needed showers in his room. Successful once, these brazen Brits then returned daily, just to wash up.

So when freelancer Al Goodman showed up one morning to interview Bogart, the Greenpeace spokesman knew just what to expect. "Another freelancer?" he asked. "You're here for a shower, too?"

6 WAR ZONE

It all happened quickly. Four cars waited in line at the roadblock, and the Chechen guards were beating up the driver of the first car. Steve LeVine, a contract super-stringer for *The New York Times* on his way to the town of Urus Martan, knew better than to get involved; one doesn't provoke angry soldiers bearing grenade launchers. So he sat tight in his car, alert.

A correspondent who had freelanced his way around the world, LeVine was experienced in war zones. He had covered communist guerrillas in the Philippines, the Tamil Tigers in Sri Lanka, and Islamic mujahadeen in the mountains of Afghanistan. These Chechen fighters, the wooden shack, and the bar blocking the road were just like many others he had encountered, in this war and elsewhere. Common sense, a cool head, and caution would see him through the situation safely.

His traveling companions—another Western correspondent and a Georgian journalist—got out of the car. Who knew how long they might have to wait? Still apprehensive but getting restless, LeVine got out, too. Fluent in Russian, he struck up a conversation with a nervous Chechen soldier dressed in winter camouflage—mottled white, to blend with snow—and carrying a rocket-propelled grenade launcher. Everybody kept a watchful eye on the nearby scuffle.

Suddenly the conflict escalated, and the soldier in white wheeled around, yelling angrily in Chechen. He raised the grenade launcher to his shoulder, aimed at the driver, and fired.

Only ten feet away, the deafening back-blast from the grenade launcher knocked LeVine and his companions to the ground. "It was like an earthquake," LeVine said.

Momentarily unable to hear, LeVine struggled to rise from the hard pavement. His left leg—shattered at the shin from the blast—bent inward and collapsed. "You could see everything. A fist-sized piece of flesh was gone just above the ankle, tendons were exposed, and blood was puddling," he recalled. "I immediately went into shock."

Miles from combat, not even a party to the conflict at hand, LeVine had just become a casualty of the Chechen uprising, another journalist injured—nearly killed—covering a war.

WARS ARE RISKIER FOR STRINGERS

In the popular imagination, foreign correspondence is often synonymous with war correspondence. Indeed, various well-known journalists got their start in the trenches, some as freelancers. Covering violent conflicts in distant lands is inevitably difficult, dangerous work, certainly for staff correspondents—as portrayed so dramatically in films such as *The Killing Fields* and *The Year of Living Dangerously*—and possibly even more so for stringers.

A primary reason is cost; operating in a war zone can be extremely expensive, and without a major news organization to foot the bill most reporters cannot afford to operate effectively or safely.

For instance, transportation costs can cripple a freelancer on a limited budget. During the height of the Chechen conflict in January and February of 1995, independent drivers were charging journalists operating from outlying villages between $300 and $400 per day for transport to and from nearby

Grozny, the capital of the breakaway republic. Freelancers getting paid $150–$200 per story usually cannot afford such fees, let alone pay $700 per day to rent armored vehicles, which major media sometimes do if they haven't bought the vehicle outright. Hitching a ride is okay, but ultimately hit or miss. Without ready access to transportation, it can become very difficult to chase down stories.

WAR IN THE BALKANS

Despite such challenges, some determined and resourceful freelancers can and do work well from war zones, filing for major media. Todd Bensman operated on an extremely low budget covering the Balkan crisis.

Based in Prague, Bensman had developed steady income from work at *The Prague Post*, as well as from several trade strings for which he wrote regularly. Soon, seeking more compelling stories and better clips, he decided to travel to Zagreb, and from there to cover fighting that was spreading throughout the region.

At that time, Canadian peacekeeping troops were scheduled for deployment in Croatia, and Bensman, while still in Prague, successfully pitched a story on their arrival to Canadian Press & Broadcast News. He also contacted editors at several newspapers to inform them of his destination.

Calculating his operating expenses for a three-week trip, Bensman changed $250 into German Deutschmarks, the currency he had been advised would serve him best in the region. With notebooks, a camera, his laptop, and a file of background clips in his backpack, he boarded the train for Zagreb.

Serendipitously, he struck up a friendship with a fellow traveler, a Croatian music professor who happened to have an extra apartment in Zagreb. Not only did Bensman line up free housing, he gained an invaluable source of information. The professor was an intelligent, articulate, and informed local glad to be of help to a young American journalist.

Once in Zagreb, Bensman presented a letter of introduction from the *Seattle Times* to the government press office and was issued proper press credentials. Taking the Croatian equivalent of Greyhound, he then made his way toward the front, hitching a ride with Croatian soldiers the last few miles into Pakrac, a town being demolished by house-to-house fighting between Serbs and Croats.

It was a picture of devastation: buildings bombed out, walls riddled with bullet holes, the gunfire crackling and mortars booming still filling the air. Entering a bunker, the Croatians introduced him to a twenty-three-year-old militia leader called Commander Gonzo. A soldier who spoke English translated. "They were all sort of laughing at me, because I was green," Bensman said. Did he want to see some fighting? they asked. Bensman said yes—he wanted to get some "color," news parlance for dramatic, firsthand information rich in imagery.

So they got in a car and drove toward the fighting. Drawing close, they piled out of the car and began a harried dash for cover. "We had to run from building to building. We were in the middle of it all. There was shooting everywhere." Making their way to the fifth floor of an apartment building-turned-fortress, Bensman and his escorts entered a darkened room where soldiers, ankle-deep in shell casings, stood at every window, firing at Serbs some fifty yards away.

"It was just deafening," Bensman recalled. But the soldiers, almost casually, would step away from their positions to share their thoughts about the impending Canadian deployment and the impact these peacekeepers might have on the fighting.

Story in hand, Bensman made his way out and back to Zagreb. Banging out three articles on his laptop, which he had left at his new friend's apartment, he filed to Canadian Press & Broadcast News and beat out the Canadian staff correspondents, who had just begun to arrive in town. One story didn't sell, but two did—for a total of $300. Mission accomplished.

"At the time I was exultant," Bensman said. "I had gotten paid for a freelance piece from a war zone. That was a coup. I didn't care about the money; I just wanted to cover the expenses of the trip." He had, with a $50 surplus to boot.

Baptized by fire, Bensman would go on to cover combat regularly for the next two years, but said in retrospect that his first story in Pakrac didn't justify the danger. "I *believe* in that kind of reporting, but only when it's a very strategic battle or there's a very key event that somebody needs to see, to confirm. In this case it was gratuitous," he said. "They were taking an apartment building that didn't have any significance in the war."

AT THE FRONT IN ANGOLA
. . . .

Margaret Knox once took a trip to Cuito, Angola, for just such a firsthand, proof-positive story. Cuito, a city in central Angola that became a symbolic trophy as it traded hands throughout that country's twenty-year civil war, was virtually impossible for journalists to reach without official assistance. News about its occupation was consequently hard to verify.

The Cuban-backed Angolan government, in an effort to convince the world it was winning the fight against rebel UNITA forces, decided to fly a group of Western reporters into Cuito to prove that the government did indeed control the area.

Knox had heard about the trip through colleagues in Harare, Zimbabwe, and had applied at the Angolan embassy for a spot on the plane. Permission came at the last possible moment, and she rushed to the airport. Once in Angola she met up with other journalists, and a government cargo plane flew them into the region. On the ground only briefly, she then clambered into the glass bubble of a small, roaring helicopter for the next leg of the journey. Landing again, she climbed aboard a groaning, cumbersome military truck that churned up clouds of red dust as it carried her to yet another junction, where an armored personnel carrier finally showed up, hours later, to ferry her and the others into Cuito proper.

"It was like a ghost town," she says, describing the old colonial downtown area. Once-pastel buildings now looked grim and abandoned, and the debris of shelling was everywhere. The poor outskirts were more active, with cook-fires burning outside thatched huts, goats grazing amidst scrub, and children playing. "People were going about their daily lives, and being shelled several times a day."

The army major in charge announced a news conference, and the group followed him out onto a suspension bridge to hear how the government was winning the war—"inspired propaganda," as Knox saw it. The bridge, made of chain and slats of wood, was sagging precariously from recent bombing. There was no railing, and gaping holes exposed the river below. Bunkers lined the riverbanks and soldiers with automatic weapons looked on curiously. "You watched your step," Knox said.

Her tape recorder was on when the first shell hit, sending up a flash, a cloud of smoke, and dust, followed by a deep, resonating boom "that you could feel in the bridge under your feet."

"Everybody ran, including the major. 'Get off! Go! Get out of there!' he yelled. Everybody knew the bridge was the target." Knox and the others ran, as harried soldiers hustled them as quickly as possible back into the armored personnel carrier, which lurched off on the long trip home. It was all on tape, from the major's speech to the exploding shells to her own labored breathing as she dashed across the swaying, dilapidated bridge to safety.

Back at the airstrip, waiting for the transport to take off, a peddler arrived with a basket of big red apples. Famished, she ate several. "I forgot basic safety," she said. Unwashed, the fruit worked like a laxative. It was not a pleasant trip home.

Professionally the journey was worth it. The speech cut short by the sound of exploding shells made for riveting audio on National Public Radio. The story was one of strategic importance.

HOW CLOSE TO THE FRONT IS CLOSE ENOUGH?

Steve LeVine sums up battle coverage this way: "There are very few stories at the front. Most of the stories you want to write are at the back; they're about the impact on people, about soldiers, about strategy. You don't have to put yourself in danger ninety-nine percent of the time."

Freelance TV cameraman Henry Bautista is more to the point. He's covered hot spots for the American networks for twenty years and has lost three colleagues to violent conflicts. "Don't risk your life," he advises. "It's not worth it."

The motivations that drive freelance war correspondents to put themselves in such potentially dangerous situations are several and complex. Some are highly personal, some professional. Todd Bensman, like many journalists, did so for career reasons.

"It was obvious that jobs at the larger papers were rare and pretty hard to come by. I'm white, male, and don't have an Ivy League education, and felt I had to do something extraordinary so I could get into an editor's face sometime. Something that couldn't be ignored. So I picked war."

This strategy, while dangerous, has for many people proven effective over the years. "Freelancing in hot spots has always been the fastest way up," said Alan Riding. It happened with Vietnam in the 1960s, then Central America in the 1970s and 1980s, and Bosnia in the 1990s, not to mention other wars. Armed conflicts have served as springboards for many careers.

One recent example is that of Kit Roane, a *New York Times* freelancer in Los Angeles who left that position to freelance from Sarajevo and soon was filing regularly on the Bosnian conflict for the *Times*.

"If he'd gone to New York—become a clerk, tried the reporter training program, worked on Metro—it would have taken ten years" to get overseas, said Riding.

But Ric MacInnes Rae, a staff correspondent for Canadian Broadcasting Corporation radio who's covered Bosnia, Chechnya, and other wars, said full-timers and freelancers ought to ask themselves why they take assignments in a war zone. He believes that the main reason should be to work as an impartial witness to the conflict, to tell the story. MacInnes Rae said he's seen too many of what he calls "mercenaries" among the press, those who go principally to flirt with danger and improve their careers.

Recalling the slew of reporters who covered American involvement in Vietnam, stringer Seymour Hersh stands out. He was a freelancer when he exposed the My Lai massacre, an event so shocking it helped shift the tide of American public opinion against the war. Hersh also won a Pulitzer Prize for his work.

Winning a Pulitzer Prize is of course the exception. Sometimes just filing any story is an accomplishment worthy of recognition, especially for freelancers in areas without reliable telephone lines. In some situations, satellite phones are the only way to file to the outside world, and portable units capable of transmitting voice, fax, and modem communication can cost tens of thousands of dollars. Unfortunately, even if a freelancer can borrow access to such equipment, filing can become prohibitively expensive at transmission rates of at least $20 per minute.

Consider the communications headaches of Todd Bensman's monthlong trip to Moldova in 1992, where rebel Russian Cossack units were fighting the Romanian majority to establish a breakaway republic. After a difficult train journey through the Ukraine to reach rebel forces, he discovered that most phone lines had been severed, making it impossible to file via voice or modem. Ever resourceful, Bensman borrowed a local insurance company's computer and printer to generate written copy that he sent out with departing reporters. The copy was never delivered. "I scammed on everyone and I didn't sell a word, not a single word. Didn't get a dime out of it."

Bensman admitted that he overestimated American media interest in the conflict, but said that much of the problem was timeliness. Unable to file quickly, his stories got stale.

Worse yet, Bensman nearly lost his life when a sniper's bullet missed his head by inches. It was a careless moment. He was sitting on the edge of a trench during a lull in the fighting, enjoying the sun. "It sounded like a loud snap," he said, describing the bullet that whizzed past his ear. "It put the fear of God into me."

TAKING THE NECESSARY PRECAUTIONS

This incident—and that of LeVine in Chechnya—serve as chilling reminders of the extreme danger involved in war correspondence. Money can buy some protection. The shopping list should start with bullet-proof vests, which are a must for anyone planning to go near the front lines. Some of the vests most popular with professionals are those sold by **RBR Armour** in London, England (telephone 44-171-703-1005). This company makes its vest of Kevlar (a synthetic material), which it claims is capable of stopping a bullet from a Kalashnikov assault rifle fired at ten yards. Models with neck and genital guards offer the most protection. Flak jackets, widely available from security firms, military surplus, and police supply stores in the United States, also help prevent potentially deadly shrapnel wounds. Helmets are another vital precaution, yet the cost of a good helmet and flak jacket can easily reach $2,000.

Stringers working without the full logistical backing of major media rarely enjoy the material support that CNN's staff correspondent in Brussels, Patricia Kelly, received on two occasions when CNN decided to send her and camera crews into combat zones in the former Yugoslavia. Kelly, whose career included fourteen years as a freelancer, already had a helmet and flak jacket but her three-member crews did not. She phoned Atlanta to ask for help, and CNN's London bureau shipped the necessary gear to Brussels within hours. "I wouldn't dream of asking anyone to go into a dangerous situation if they didn't have protection" and appropriate insurance, Kelly said. Not that health insurance or safety equipment guarantees safety. Steve LeVine was wearing both a helmet and flak jacket when he was seriously wounded at the Chechen roadblock.

Language skills are also paramount, not just to get the story but to save your life. Lawrence Sheets was in charge of a Reuters TV crew when bandits waylaid them on a remote road in the Caucasus Mountains and forced them from their car at gunpoint. Absolutely everything was taken. Fortunately, Sheets' fluent Russian saved them from injury, perhaps even death. Later, walking to the next village, Sheets had the good fortune to run into a local warlord whom he'd featured recently in a story. Informed of the robbery, the warlord saw to it that the car and TV equipment were promptly returned.

Years earlier and an ocean away, freelancer Caitlin Randall's good Spanish enabled her to understand the danger she and a Reuters photographer faced while accompanying a patrol of Contra fighters in southern Nicaragua. "We heard gunfire up ahead," she recalled, and her escorts began to argue. "The Contras had no idea what they were doing. They were these bumbling kids. We knew we'd better save ourselves because these bozos weren't going to." She and the photographer persuaded a few Contras to accompany them back to the nearby river, which they crossed by boat to safety in Costa Rica.

If you don't speak the pertinent local language, you will have to rely on an interpreter to help you do your job. This can be constricting, especially in smaller conflicts where governments or armed groups control what is often a small pool of available translators. It can also become expensive.

So if you are considering freelancing from a war zone, think it through carefully. Even if you can afford the communications costs and necessary safety equipment, do you have an in-depth knowledge of the region or conflict? What do you really have to offer that will make your stories better than the next reporter's?

NPR's Sylvia Poggioli said she met "too many stringers" during the Bosnian conflict who were "in a dangerous situation and didn't always have the background to cover the story."

Remember, a willingness to take risks is not enough. Sheets argues that taking risks bears little relationship to journalistic results. "I've known journalists who take a minimum number of risks and still do a very effective job of covering wars. I've also known journalists who seem to put themselves at risk all the time and end up getting minimum benefit. Obviously the level of danger increases depending on what kinds of risks one takes."

BASIC SAFETY TIPS

There are some steps that reporters can take to minimize risks while working in a war zone. The following are gleaned from reporters in the field and from the *War Correspondents Survival Guide*, an excellent publication by the Committee to Protect Journalists that should be reviewed thoroughly by anyone considering war correspondence.

- Always attempt to obtain the proper accreditation before working in a war zone. Such accreditation could spell the difference between liberty and a firing squad. Before entering a war zone, consult with the Committee to Protect Journalists in New York at (212) 465-1004 for region-specific recommendations.

- Avoid riding in the back seat of two-door automobiles because two-door models are hard to get out of quickly. Relatively speaking, they are far more dangerous than four-door models in areas where the vehicle can take hits from firearms, shrapnel, and other projectiles.

- Avoid riding in military vehicles in combat zones, as they can readily become targets.

- Avoid wearing military-issue clothing or carrying military gear, however practical. You do not wish to be mistaken for a soldier.

- Avoid driving on gravel or dirt roads, where belligerents can easily plant hidden land mines. Also, avoid driving at night.

- Do not travel alone in combat zones or areas of potential strife. Moving about with a colleague or partner is safer. This is true for several reasons. One is judgment: two minds are usually better than one in evaluating any given situation. Also, in times of imminent danger, four eyes are better than two. Having said that, choose your partner carefully. You don't want Rambo, and neither do you want someone who will panic at the first sign of trouble.

  Traveling with a partner also tends to reduce the possibility that you will be robbed. Remember, people living or fighting in war zones can become quite desperate and irrational. Even small sums of money or simple material goods may provide enough incentive for robbery—even murder—when the perpetrator knows there will be no legal repercussions.

FACING SUSPICIOUS LOCALS
· ·

In extended conflicts, locals often begin to suspect that journalists are spying for one side or another. As Lawrence Sheets recalls the situation in Chechnya, the warm welcome he and other Western journalists received at the outset of the conflict quickly faded.

"Months of Russian bombing left villagers who had lost family and friends convinced that foreign correspondents were giving away the coordinates of their homes and reporting on the strategic situation in the area to the Russian military," Sheets says. "Some Chechen rebels also came to believe that their positions were being disclosed to the Russians by unscrupulous journalists."

The claims were absurd, but in one instance an Azerbaijani cameraman working alone for Associated Press TV was executed behind Chechen lines, apparently because his captors thought he was working for the Russian security services. Perhaps they just wanted his video camera. Whatever the reason, some other correspondents believe the tragedy might have been avoided had he been traveling with a partner.

Local suspicions toward Western journalists—staff and freelance—can also be inflamed by outrageous public comments such as those of former Central Intelligence Agency director John Deutch. In 1996 he said the CIA might post spies abroad posing as foreign correspondents, a despicable tactic used in the past. Deutch later backtracked somewhat, stating that he would send spies posing as journalists only in "genuinely extraordinary" circumstances. Subsequently, Congress passed legislation banning the use of bona fide U.S. journalists as spies except with presidential approval.

If you are working in a war zone and find yourself accused of spying, your life may depend on your ability to convince belligerents or angry locals of your true status.

When dealing with belligerents, it is imperative to know

their attitudes toward your respective nationality and the area from which you've just come. Even in the smallest wars and conflicts, opposing sides usually have passionate feelings about your government's foreign policy. A good rule of thumb is to turn this passion to your benefit if belligerents share your government's policy outlook, and, conversely, make it clear that you and your government are two different entities if the official line is a liability. With a little diplomacy, you can do this without expressing outright sympathy for one side or another or compromising your integrity.

Keep in mind that working in war zones may require a certain amount of lip service to governmental and quasi-governmental bodies. It can save you from suspicion, harassment, or possible detention. You may also find yourself spending relatively long periods of time listening to propagandistic diatribes. Just be patient if not obsequious, as difficult as it may seem. Simple nods may open doors later that could make a story or perhaps even save your life.

When reporting one side's accounts of victory in a given battle or the atrocities of its enemies, you should qualify your reports, if possible with the other side's viewpoint. Refugees can be a good source of information but are notorious for exaggerating accounts of barbarism which they themselves may have gotten through hearsay. There is a simple rule that many correspondents follow: if you can get refugees to provide firsthand accounts with names, dates, and times, then the information is worth using. If not, chances are that the information has been handed down to them and distorted in the process.

War reporting *can* be very rewarding. It may occasionally lead to a big break with a major publication or news organization if a particular outfit lacks a correspondent in the right place at the right time and you—a talented freelancer—are there to fill the gap.

South African freelancer Phillip van Niekerk got two front-page bylines in *The New York Times* in April 1996 when the civil war in Liberia flared up and he was hunkering down in a beachfront hotel near the besieged U.S. embassy in the capital of Monrovia. Fighting had damaged the airport, preventing a *Times* staffer from arriving. Van Niekerk, already on contract for *The Observer* of London, knew the *Times*'s foreign editor from previous stories and had access to a working phone line; seizing the opportunity, he was soon reporting on the American evacuation from the capital of hundreds of U.S. citizens and other nationals.

But don't count on any lucky breaks. If you do decide to report from a war zone, you need to make excellent professional contacts before you land in-country. That means a solid commitment from at least one news outlet to buy your stories. Remember to talk with them up front about logistics and expenses, including the cost of safety equipment.

In addition, don't forget to purchase a health insurance policy that covers you in a war zone. Sylvia Poggioli was an NPR stringer when she started covering the conflict in Yugoslavia. Reporting from Slovenia, she came under shelling. "I called NPR and said 'I'm not filing another story unless you get me war insurance.'" NPR followed through.

In its survival guide for journalists working in the former Yugoslavia, the Committee to Protect Journalists states unequivocally: "Freelancers: if you can't handle the cost and logistics of insurance, you can't handle the cost and logistics of a bullet wound. Revise your plans."

On balance, we advise against freelancing in a war zone, especially if you are inexperienced. Covering armed conflicts is dangerous work, even if you are street-smart and very careful. In 1995 alone, fifty-one journalists were killed while covering wars or by repressive authorities, according to the Committee to Protect Journalists.

The sad truth is that you don't have to do something foolhardy to get seriously hurt or killed as a war correspondent. Paul McGorrian, 27, quit the *St. Petersburg Times* in Florida to become a freelancer in Pakistan, setting up shop in the capital,

Islamabad. The Dartmouth College graduate planned to cover the war and its refugee problem in neighboring Afghanistan for several clients, including his former newspaper and CBS Network Radio News.

As Steve LeVine tells it, bad luck followed McGorrian like a plague. "He was trying to make it, full of energy and ideas," LeVine said, but McGorrian contracted hepatitis almost immediately, which laid him flat in a local hospital. After a difficult recovery, the stringer flew to Lahore to pursue a story but was robbed at gunpoint on arrival and lost everything. Discouraged but not defeated, he pulled himself together and set out once again to get that coveted first clip. Following a lead, he boarded a plane at the town of Gilgit, in northern Pakistan, home of the mountain K2. The plane took off for the 45-minute flight to Islamabad, but disappeared without a trace. The stringer was never found.

TRAVELING WHILE WOUNDED
· ·

LeVine was much luckier. Though he was seriously injured by the grenade launcher blast, he had colleagues who were able to rush him from the roadblock back to a Grozny hospital funded by the international medical relief group Médecins sans Frontières. Unlike many medical facilities in that part of the world, this one had an X-ray machine, antibiotics, and a good doctor—everything necessary to temporarily patch him up for a painful, half-day road trip in a van making its way out of Chechnya.

Throughout the emergency, *The New York Times* spared no expense to help LeVine. Worried about his medical treatment in Grozny but unable to airlift him out of there, the *Times* hired an air ambulance to fly down from Moscow to meet the van carrying him at an airstrip near the Chechen border. It was a small twin-engine prop; the green canvas stretcher to which LeVine was strapped had to be tilted sideways to fit through the door. He grimaced and hung on. Once in Moscow, the

Times put him on a first-class flight back to the United States for surgery—a race against the clock as the wound was nearly a week old by that time, and doctors were concerned about the mangled bones setting badly.

"If somebody's working in a dangerous place for *The New York Times*, then we consider it a moral obligation to take care of them," *Times* foreign editor Bill Keller explained later. "It's really self-defeating to abandon someone in time of danger. The message to other reporters is that reporters are expendable." Unfortunately, not all media are so generous to freelancers, so be careful. You might not get any help at all.

Back in Inglewood, California, surgeons set LeVine's ankle with two metal halos, high-tension wires, and four metal rods. On crutches for months, LeVine slowly regained mobility.

Finally, after nine long months LeVine went back into action overseas, though he was still uncertain of his recovery. On one of his earliest assignments in the field, reporting for *Newsweek* in Afghanistan, LeVine and three other Western correspondents had to take cover behind a low mud wall as mortars rained in from Islamic Taliban fundamentalists battling nearby Afghan troops. Sprinting past long, dangerous gaps in the wall as he approached the front lines, LeVine felt no weakness in the leg. "It was the first time I had run since the injury," he recalled. "I was very pleased."

He says his injury in Chechnya was just a fluke accident, that no one could have foreseen or prevented it. He believes a similar fluke killed a freelancer he knew: twenty-eight-year-old American photographer Cynthia Elbaum, who died in a Russian air raid on a residential area near Grozny on December 22, 1994. Out photographing damage from the previous day's raid, she was caught in the wrong place at the wrong time. "It was her first war assignment," LeVine remembered. "She arrived on Saturday and was killed on Thursday. There was no way of knowing." The Chechens, moved by Elbaum's sacrifice, named a square after her.

7 BACK IN THE NEWSROOM

The world looks different from back in the newsroom, and editors and producers are generally cautious when dealing with stringers they don't know well. Freelance foreign correspondents have to earn the trust of these distant colleagues, and communicating clearly is vital to this undertaking. Failure to do so, however unintentional, can have serious consequences.

Consider the case of a *New York Times* stringer in a Latin American country who thought there'd be a scoop in a rare interview with the country's controversial president. During the interview, the president let slip a political secret. The *Times* ran the story and it got a lot of attention, but not the kind the stringer wanted.

For starters, the president immediately branded the story false. That brought out a pack of local journalists demanding to know the *Times*'s response to the president's allegations. But the biggest problems were with the foreign desk back in New York, which the stringer did not inform until it was too late. "I don't mind big scandals," said *New York Times* foreign editor Bill Keller, "but I'd like to know they're coming."

The stringer's judgment had fallen short on two counts. First, the stringer failed to contact the desk before conducting this very important interview, precluding editors from calling the relevant staff correspondent whose beat included the country in question. It also looked like a case of turf-jumping, because as it turned out the staff correspondent had been trying to line up the same interview for weeks, but was out of the country when the stringer got in to see the president.

Second, in defending the story to the local press, the stringer produced a tape of the interview, but again without first contacting the foreign desk. In what was turning into a major local dispute, the stringer unwisely assumed the role of de facto spokesperson for the *Times*.

In the end, the stringer salvaged professional credibility because the tape proved that the article had not in fact distorted the words of the president, whose bluster was just a forceful attempt at political damage control. "It did help that the story was right," Keller said.

Unfortunately, the stringer's relationship with the *Times* was strained, even if only temporarily. The reporter could have avoided upsetting the editors with a few timely phone calls to the desk. News organizations like the *Times* insist on close coordination between the newsroom and distant stringers. "I want people rowing in the same direction," Keller said.

He's not alone. Concise, straightforward communication is the foundation of a successful partnership between freelance foreign correspondents and their colleagues back in the newsroom. "The main rule," offered Jim Handman, former foreign editor at Canadian Broadcasting Corporation radio, "is you don't want your editor to be surprised."

BUILDING TRUST AND
LEARNING THE PECKING ORDER
. . . .

As a freelance foreign correspondent, you are an important source of information for editors and producers, especially so

if your client relies primarily or exclusively on stringers to provide coverage in your country or region. But even if you are a
key source of stories, it's worth remembering that newsrooms
typically view stringers differently than they do staffers, particularly at the outset of your working relationship.

Why? News organizations fight hard to maintain their integrity and professionalism, and they want to feel confident
about who is working for them. Freelancers can gain that confidence by communicating well with the newsroom from the
outset, sowing seeds of trust and cultivating them with dili-
gence.

"The initial trust is much more tentative" for the stringer
than the staffer, Keller said. "Trust is built up over time." ABC-
TV foreign editor Chuck Lustig says it's only natural for newsrooms to think this way. "We trust staff correspondents. We
rely on them. We train them and place them."

Yet as a freelance foreign correspondent, you can forge very
strong links with client newsrooms. It may take longer to build
up trust at certain outfits because, like any group of professionals, foreign correspondents have their own hierarchy. At
the top of the heap are staff correspondents for the networks
and major papers, including *The New York Times*, *The Wall
Street Journal*, *The Washington Post*, and the *Los Angeles Times*.
At the bottom of the heap are freelancers.

Frequently, the bigger the media, the lower the freelancers
are on the "food chain." Some newsrooms, reported one editor,
even view stringers "as creatures from a lower caste." Don't let
this get you down; any freelancer who consistently does top-
notch work can slay such prejudice quickly. Yet recognizing
that there is a pecking order and discerning your place in it,
however temporary, is essential to understanding your editors
and their attitude toward your work. You may be very important in one organization, less so at the next.

Major media, including *The New York Times*, *Business Week*,
NPR, CNN, ABC-TV, and others, tend to separate their nonstaff

reporters into categories. At the top are "contract" employees who get a salary but not necessarily all the fringe benefits. This is as close as one can come to being on staff without actually having the status of a full-time employee. Below that are reporters who may get monthly retainers, day rates, or word rates. Next come stringers who are paid strictly on a piece-by-piece basis.

Wire services operate a little differently. For example, Associated Press staff correspondents hired in the United States before being sent abroad generally enjoy better pay, better benefits, and—some insiders say—greater professional status than AP full-timers hired abroad. Part-time stringers hired locally earn still less money. Contract or not, any freelancer who works regularly for a blue-chip news outlet usually commands an extra measure of respect from freelance colleagues. On the flip side, wannabes who hang out at the local press center but rarely file are considered "bottom feeders."

Major media place staff foreign correspondents in certain key cities. Some give contracts to reporters in secondary locations. National Public Radio, for example, has staff bureaus in London, Cairo, Tokyo, Hong Kong, Nairobi, Mexico City, Rome, and Moscow. It has contract reporters in Jerusalem, Frankfurt, Abidjan, and Brazil, and turns to piece-work stringers in other locations.

Freelancers are by nature a mobile bunch, and opportunities to move up are quite common. Just do good work, stay alert, and be ready.

COMMUNICATING WITH EDITORS
AND GIVING THEM WHAT THEY WANT

How much contact should you have with your editors? It depends on your importance to a particular newsroom, and that may change quickly if a big story lands on your doorstep.

Turkey-based freelancer Andrew Finkel is not an everyday presence on CNN but he was on the phone with CNN producers practically nonstop after terrorists sympathetic to Chechen rebels hijacked a Russian passenger ferry and threatened to sink it in the Bosporus straits, near Istanbul. He was CNN's man on the scene for more than 24 hours, until a staff correspondent could get there to take over. CNN senior producer Rob Golden said that freelancers "are able to fill that precious gap of time from the moment a story breaks until we can corral our resources and send staffers in there."

Daily, weekly, or hourly communication may be appropriate with your media, depending on the story at hand and how frequently they disseminate news.

Advertising Age, which relies almost exclusively on freelancers for coverage outside North America, offers an electronic product called the *Daily World Wire* featuring short news items that stringers file by e-mail. Consequently, some stringers may contact editors five days a week, if they've got news to report. Or they might file once a week. John Pollack, in Madrid, spoke with the *Miami Herald* only once every few months, usually when a Cuban defector landed in Spain.

Editors and producers want you to contact them if you have significant news to report or stories to pitch. But if all's quiet on the western front, you probably should be, too. Your knowledge of your media's needs and your best news sense must serve as a guide.

Keep in mind that if a particular news outlet relies primarily on staff correspondents or wire services for overseas coverage, your conversations with editors and producers are likely to be shorter and less frequent. A good rule for foreign freelancers is to make a quick, concise pitch and never prolong the conversation unless it's at the editor's initiative. Back in the newsroom, editors often give a low priority to dealing with stringers. But don't be shy. "Too many stringers are passive, just waiting for the assignment," said Stewart Toy, *Business*

Week's former bureau chief in Paris. If you have a good story idea, send an e-mail or make a quick call. While editors and producers might be too busy to solicit stories (or simply be unaware of what's going on in your country), they will often take good story ideas that come in over the transom. "If somebody calls with a really good idea, we'll take a look at it," said *USA Today*'s John Simpson. "I like it when people send me information that shows they're keeping abreast of things," added *USA Today*'s Elisa Tinsley. "It lets me know I should be thinking of stories in their region."

Don't be a pest, either. CNN senior producer Rob Golden recounted the story of one stringer in Panama who was too persistent. "She would call us and give us tips; that was helpful. But it got to the point of calling in every little detail about Panama, which we didn't really need. It got to the point where we didn't take her seriously." Then one day a politically motivated shooting occurred in Panama, and CNN needed her to write a voice-track to accompany footage that Atlanta already had in hand. "I can still remember the first line of the track," Golden said. "'It was a beautiful day in Panama . . .' She couldn't write for broadcast or print."

Sometimes even good story ideas get shot down; tight budgets, limited space, and other pressing stories often take their toll. Don't get discouraged. Bill Keller of *The New York Times* said, "Stringers need to be thick-skinned, which means patient, humble, but persistent, and ready to take 'no' for an answer."

This is especially so at blue-chip media, where it can be tough for a freelance foreign correspondent to register on a busy editor's radar screen. Even when a stringer succeeds in getting a face-to-face meeting with an editor in a newsroom, holding their attention can be a difficult art. Al Goodman has been in various newsrooms pitching story ideas he thought were fabulous, only to hear an editor reply, "Hmmm. Excuse me, I've got to take a phone call." The trick is to stay on track for those often brief moments between distractions. That's when an editor may finally assign some stories.

After making a pitch, freelancers should be ready to spring into action when an editor or producer gives a "green light" to the story idea. Freelancing is all about seizing opportunities you help create. So it's useful to pay close attention to the types of stories a particular news outlet is seeking, and in what format they want them delivered. "Read the publication and understand its peculiarities," advised *The Christian Science Monitor*'s Clayton Jones. "Does it like a lot of quotes? What range of story lengths? Color? Analysis? How much sourcing?" While most editors and producers don't expect stringers to know their medium's news style as intimately as a staffer working there fifty or sixty hours a week, they learn quickly which freelancers make an effort to deliver polished work on time.

"I just don't have time to play around with bad copy and people who miss deadline," said *USA Today*'s Tinsley. "I'm not expecting a Pulitzer Prize–winning piece from somebody who's just landed, but I do expect them to cover their bases."

As foreign editor of the *Miami Herald*, Juan Tamayo always put a premium on "good stringers who could write quickly and write to measure." If an editor asks for a 1,500-word story, aim to hit the target, sending the requested length. If a radio producer likes a certain type of actuality—interviews recorded on tape, for instance—chase them down for your spots. Listen closely to the newsroom's instructions, and always use the pertinent lingo. When a TV producer tells you he wants to see some good "b-roll" he's not referring to a circus trick. He wants engaging news footage. If you're told to keep the cuts straightforward in the two-minute package, or to remain still during your standup on camera, do so.

Remember, editors and producers usually have myriad story options among wire services, syndicates, staff correspondents, and stringers. The material you deliver has to be fresh and insightful. In the age of the global electronic village, simply translating the local news just doesn't pass muster.

CBC's Jim Handman said he's been amazed by the number of inexperienced stringers who called to pitch a "breaking" news story a day after it's been on the wires. "It raises questions about their aggressiveness. If they're smart, they do a second-day story," he noted.

Tinsley agreed. "The key is to find stories that the wires are not covering." Amidst the flood of articles on the AIDS epidemic, one freelancer wowed her with a piece from Kenya on an ethical debate raging there among American expatriates: Should you or shouldn't you test your housekeeper, maid, or nanny for the virus that causes AIDS?

As the "Nannies and AIDS" story illustrates, finding an American angle for an American publication can make the difference between landing an assignment or not. The same goes for Canadian and British media, which want stories relevant to their particular audiences. You might sell a story based on its hometown angle, its straight news punch, or because the story shows how events in one country fit into a broader regional or global trend. The trick, not always easy, is finding the right angle.

When pitching stories, it's important to be aware of client media's daily schedules. When do editors or producers meet to discuss the content of the next edition or broadcast? What are the daily deadlines? If you have a story idea and it's not breaking news, call well before the meeting, and not right at deadline when key editors and producers are likely to be very busy.

BEFRIENDING BIGFOOT: HOW TO WORK WITH STAFF CORRESPONDENTS

When a staff correspondent for a major paper or network comes to town, the local stringer who works for that news outlet generally gets "big-footed"—squeezed out of the Big Story. The term is descriptive; staffers automatically have first choice of the stories they want to cover, and stringers who work for their media had better not stand in the way, or they'll get stepped on. Clayton Jones speaks for a lot of editors and producers when he says, "We want to reserve good stories for the staffer." So don't be surprised when it happens to you, and don't get upset. Working with visiting staff foreign correspondents is a great opportunity that smart freelancers will take advantage of without hesitation.

While it may seem unfair that roving staff correspondents often jet in to cover the best stories and leave you with the sidebars, building a good relationship with them can pay great dividends in the long run. First, you can learn more about a particular news outlet by working closely with their staffers and about journalism in general. Cooperating with them also helps build stronger relationships with editors and producers back home, developing the professional network that can lead to other jobs.

So if a staff correspondent needs your help to set up interviews, research a story, translate, or make hotel reservations, leap to it with enthusiasm. Make yourself invaluable. Share your knowledge, your contacts, and do anything you can to be helpful. Make their job easier, "even if you have to swallow your pride," said Alan Riding of *The New York Times*. Giving help grudgingly "really is a stupid approach," he added. If the staffer ends up writing a front-page story about your country, it only serves to boost the importance of your country and make your work more marketable in the future.

Never try to outfox a staff reporter, even if you know more about a particular story. "Stringers should be very careful about posing themselves as competitors with staff correspondents," said Bill Keller, who worked as a *Times* foreign correspondent in South Africa and Moscow, where he won a Pulitzer Prize in 1989 for coverage of the Soviet Union. "The quickest way to get the door slammed in your face is to antagonize the correspondent who's covering the beat. Going around them will just come back to haunt you."

Al Goodman, who covered Spain's 1993 elections on camera

for CNN, was "big-footed" in the 1996 elections when Atlanta sent in veteran staff correspondent Siobhan Darrow from London. Though understandably disappointed, Goodman hired on as a freelance field producer for Darrow and her traveling camera crew, using the opportunity to learn new techniques from more experienced pros, and earning $250 per day doing so.

Stringers will get their chance to do big stories for major media, but it's a matter of timing and working closely with staff correspondents and the staff back in the newsroom. If you gain Bigfoot's trust, he or she might not feel the immediate need to rush into your country to cover every big story; after all, you've been well trained.

JUGGLING DIFFERENT MEDIA
WHEN THINGS GET HOT

There will be times when you are in great demand and must juggle several clients' needs at once. American Mark Lavie was on contract in Israel for CBC radio and NBC radio at the outset of the Gulf War when Iraqi Scud missiles started exploding in Tel Aviv.

CBC's Jim Handman, aware that Lavie worked for NBC too, was skeptical of Lavie's ability to handle both in a crunch. Voicing his concerns, Handman said, "We both want you to go live at the top of the clock!" Lavie replied, "No problem. I can do that."

Effectively speaking, he did, and on several occasions. From his office with two phone lines, Lavie established contact with both networks, holding both phones to his ears. First, he went live for NBC on the hour for about thirty seconds, while the CBC anchors were reading the news headlines. But when he heard through the second phone that the CBC anchor was preparing to go live to Israel, Lavie concluded his brief report for NBC, smoothly mentioning the NBC anchor's name, a prearranged signal to wrap up the interview right away. Then Lavie immediately launched into a different live report for CBC. At least once, he had to switch back and forth between the two networks as the anchors peppered him with questions. "I kept waiting for him to say the wrong anchor's name," said Handman, but Lavie didn't let him down.

Less talented stringers might not be able to handle that, Handman added. For some, "two clients in a quiet situation may be too much." When faced with more work than you can handle effectively, it's important to decide quickly which clients you will serve, and in what order. Factors to consider are: how badly you need a particular string over the long run, either for steady income or for career advancement; the amount you'll be paid for the story at hand; and the professional satisfaction each job offers. After you have established these priorities in your mind, tell your editors. Don't hedge. If you don't think you can deliver a piece when an editor wants it, don't promise that you can produce for them.

"I never missed a deadline," said Elisa Tinsley, recalling her days as a stringer in the Soviet Union. "Having worked in extremely difficult situations, under onerous conditions, with people reluctant to talk, I'm a little less sympathetic to people who work in a more open climate and can't make their deadlines."

At the Bureau of National Affairs, Inc., stringers account for 5,200 stories filed each year from abroad. "We expect people to be writing for other publications," said BNA's Larry Evans. "But if the correspondent has lots of clients, we sometimes have trouble getting up the priority pole."

Evans cautions freelancers not to short-shrift editors at trade publications while chasing bylines in better-known publications like the *Los Angeles Times* or *Chicago Tribune*. "We have to compete with that glamour. What we offer is a regularity of coverage. Newspapers are in for a big story and out. Maybe they don't need the freelancer for another three months." At rates of $20–$30 per hour, a BNA stringer can earn significant income over time. Consider the freelancer who, faced with breaking news for another client right at his BNA publication's deadline, simply abandoned his commitment and failed to deliver the story he'd promised. BNA dumped him.

Too many clients, or too many clients of the same type, can cause problems for freelancers. Jim Handman said that CBC once called its stringer in the Philippines after a raging fire killed dozens of young people trapped inside a discotheque. Handman wanted the reporter to file a longer report for the network's morning news show, *World Report*. He asked what kind of sound-on-tape she had from the scene. To Handman's surprise, twelve hours after the story broke, the stringer had not yet been to the charred disco. "I've got lots of strings," she told Handman. "I had to stay home and file."

What a mistake! Handman told her it was important to be where the story was, and suggested that she ought to get a cell phone so she could file for other radio clients on the hour and still be able to record interviews and other sound elements at the scene of the blaze.

No matter how demanding your clients are you can usually satisfy them all—like Lavie did during the Scud attacks—with a little creativity and a lot of hustle.

LEAVING TOWN WITHOUT
LEAVING EDITORS IN THE LURCH

Editors and producers back in the newsroom want to know when you'll be away from your normal post and hard to contact. Give as much advance notice as possible, especially if you have stories that are finished and just awaiting a final edit back in the newsroom. Remember to tell the newsroom the day you expect to be back on duty at your normal post. "If you want them to think of you as their 'Man in Milan,' be sure to let editors know when you're away," said BNA's Evans; if you don't and an editor calls when you're away, "it leads the editor to think you could be unreliable."

Taking a minute to advise the foreign desk where you will be and how to reach you can pay unexpected dividends. Rob Golden noted that CNN might call on a stringer if there's a breaking story where he or she happens to be traveling and if the freelancer is in the best position to cover it.

Editors usually like to have the name and phone number of a backup reporter while the foreign freelancer is away (indeed, foreign freelancers sometimes fill in for staff correspondents who are away). Generally, stringers in good standing with their client media shouldn't be afraid of substitutes stealing their string. Normally, nothing the substitute can do will change your fundamental relationship with client media. As Evans said, "If there's one great story while you're gone, that's not a problem."

But not always. Many years ago, a freelancer in Madrid for an American radio network decided to join a few friends for a Sunday afternoon trip to the countryside. Normally, he'd tune in to catch the news on the radio every few hours, but this day the weather was too nice and the company too good. Shortly after he left Madrid, two 747's collided on the runway on Tenerife Island in the Canaries, a Spanish province off the coast of Africa. The carnage was incredible. More than 570 people were killed and scores injured. Oblivious to the tragedy, the stringer returned late to Madrid, turning in at three in the morning.

The ringing of an insistent phone woke him up. It was the network calling. "Anything doing in your neck of the woods?" his boss asked.

"Not that I know of," the semiconscious freelancer answered groggily.

"There's been a plane crash!" the producer yelled; the exact expletives are lost to history. He didn't fire the stringer on the spot but didn't have to, because a hungry backup stringer in Madrid had already jumped on the story—the worst crash in aviation history—and had been filing reports from the start. Worse yet, the network already had dispatched the substitute to the Canary Islands. The dejected freelancer later resigned.

Communications have improved dramatically since that 1977 incident, and today cellular phones, pagers, and voice mail can keep you in close contact with distant editors. Under normal circumstances, no editor wants to be bothered with a "going out of town" call from every freelancer taking a Sunday drive. But if you string for media that cover breaking news aggressively, it can pay to listen to the national radio news, carry a cell phone or beeper, and check your messages frequently.

Only the freelancer who's having problems with a particular editor might think twice about his or her temporary replacement. If the relationship is bad, or tenuous, you could be replaced. Because while conscientious freelancers tend to respect each others' turf, competition never really stops. Visiting staff correspondents are usually, in the back of their minds, doing a little "shopping" for new stringers who could help them in the future.

REPRESENTING YOURSELF FAIRLY TO SOURCES

If you've filed one story from abroad for the **BBC**, **NPR**, the *San Francisco Chronicle*, or the *Houston Post*, does that give you the right to go around saying you're the correspondent for that network or newspaper? No. One story does not a correspondent make, and misrepresenting yourself can seriously damage—even destroy—your working relationships with editors.

In "Guidelines for contributing to *The Christian Science Monitor*," the newspaper sets forth the following rule: "USING OUR NAME: Until we commission a story from you, you may not represent yourself to officials, sources, or credentialing authorities (or anyone else, for that matter) as a representative of

The Christian Science Monitor. Until we designate you as our stringer in a particular locality, you may not identify yourself as a *Monitor* writer in researching a prospective piece prior to pitching it to us. And you may not identify yourself as a *Monitor* writer for the purpose of obtaining a visa or a credential as a resident correspondent from a foreign government without the express written consent of the International News Editor. Obviously, once we have established a relationship, you have more leeway in identifying yourself as the *Monitor's* representative. Nonetheless we ask that you do so judiciously."

CNN's Rob Golden recalls a particularly serious case of misrepresentation in which an otherwise promising American freelancer blew her chances of becoming a CNN stringer. At an international tennis tournament in the Middle East, the stringer hired a camera crew and said she represented CNN, netting an interview with ace Boris Becker. But she made him so mad during the interview that he vowed never to talk to CNN again.

Then, during a major golf tournament, she again hired a camera crew and presented herself as a CNN reporter, producing an otherwise impressive piece but alienating producers in Atlanta who questioned her brazen assumption of CNN's backing. Angry CNN producers not only rejected her piece, they sent letters to government officials, a television station, and several other professionals in the region, alerting them all that the stringer did not represent CNN. The network also sent her a letter threatening legal action if she tried the tactic again.

The proper approach, Golden explained, would have been to contact CNN first, then make it clear to potential interview subjects that she was planning to submit the report on speculation to CNN but that it had not been commissioned. Then Boris Becker or the golf pros could have made informed decisions about whether to grant the interviews.

Honesty is the best policy. There is no shame in being a freelancer who works on speculation. You don't often need a fancy credential or big-name client to get a foot in the door. The most important thing is your self-confidence and professional demeanor. In most cases, if you act professionally, you'll be treated professionally. Remember that most people, no matter how famous, are flattered to be interviewed.

JOURNALISM ETHICS ABROAD

Most journalists, staff or freelance, pass muster when it comes to the ethics of the profession. But back in the newsroom, many editors and producers will take special care to remind stringers—even though they're not on staff—that they're expected to live up to that organization's ethical and professional standards. For stringers, avoiding even the appearance of journalistic impropriety is of paramount importance in establishing trust.

"Anything that might compromise you, let it be known," said NPR's Joyce Davis. If you sense potential conflicts of interest but do good work, editors and producers might permit you to report on certain topics while proscribing others. In one instance, an NPR journalist got into difficulty because a spouse had strong political ties and the journalist hadn't informed the newsroom. NPR severed its relationship with another stringer in Israel, Davis said, "who didn't want to do more pieces critical of the government." *The Christian Science Monitor*'s Jones put it this way: "In your heart, you're objective. But we have to deal with appearances."

At the extreme, newsrooms occasionally encounter plagiarism by unethical freelancers, who somehow fool themselves into thinking that editors back in the newsroom can't possibly catch on because they're so far removed from the story. BNA's Evans recalled one case in which a Washington editor assigned a story to a BNA stringer in Asia after reading an article in the *Financial Times*. When the stringer turned in copy, there were several paragraphs lifted straight from the *Financial Times* without attribution.

"It's an open-and-shut case," Evans said. "When we see plagiarism, we stop using the stringer." Bill Keller of the *Times* said that if a freelance reporter fails to ask key questions in an interview, or overemphasizes one aspect of a story, editors back in the newsroom can try to correct the problem. "There are mistakes that can be tolerated," he said. "But you run into a serious problem if someone doesn't know the basics of journalistic ethics."

Ethics aside, ordinary professional disagreements are bound to arise from time to time between freelance foreign correspondents and the editors back in the newsroom. Foreign correspondent Ernest Hemingway didn't always get along with his editors, and neither will you. NPR's Davis advises freelancers to be "very cooperative and not argue over an edit. It's an attitude toward the editor and the editing process. Staff has more leeway to say no." Freelancers can try to influence the editing process, but should not be uncooperative. "Otherwise, there's no incentive to work with them," she said.

Stringers will only know how far they can push for their ideas if they take realistic stock of where they stand with editors and producers back in the newsroom. The stronger the relationship, the more room there is for give-and-take. Editors say freelance foreign correspondents need to recognize that doing a few stories from the field doesn't make them an expert or qualify them to join the staff.

"They've done a couple of on-air stories for local news organizations and they think they've paid their dues," said ABC's Chuck Lustig. "Someone could be in Bosnia a few months and that doesn't mean he's ready for the network."

Yet these days newsrooms big and small need freelancers more and more, and most strive to cultivate relationships of mutual respect. "Our correspondents are our eyes and ears," said *Ad Age*'s Jan Jaben, who works regularly with about seventy-five stringers around the world. "You need to treat them with respect." To foster greater communication and a sense of community, Jaben even puts out a monthly newsletter for her far-flung corps, called *GlobaLink*. "My idea in doing this was to give them a feeling of importance, of appreciation, of being a part of something."

WHEN YOU COME HOME . . .

Most freelancers eventually return to their native countries and many get full-time jobs in one newsroom or another. Some stringers who've made the transition say that landing the staff job isn't the hardest part of returning home; culture shock is. It's often a combination of factors: a more corporate climate, a loss of independence, and a feeling that you're no longer a big fish in the pond.

"As a freelancer, you're incredibly independent. Your nearest editor might be a country away," said Laura Ballman, who freelanced in the Ukraine before returning to Atlanta for a job with CNN. "When you come back, you're one person in a big organization."

Ann Marsh returned to New York after three years in Prague, and learned her first week back of an opening at *Forbes* magazine. "I interviewed and was hired within days," Marsh said. "Far and away my most important credential was my time working abroad. Editors here tend toward a cosmopolitan world view and have hired a staff of reporters who reflect it. Most speak second or third languages. Many have lived and written from abroad. I had expected editors would scoff at my time in Europe as irrelevant to work in the U.S.—a cautionary tale oft-repeated to journalists returning to America. Thankfully, my experience was the opposite."

Freelancer Jesse Tinsley (no relation to Elisa) also landed on his feet when he returned to the United States after six years in

Spain. His former employer in Denver, the *Rocky Mountain News*, didn't hire him back, but within five months he found a job at the *Knoxville News-Sentinel*. A year later he moved up to *The Plain Dealer* in Cleveland.

Even relatively inexperienced freelancers can return home to find good jobs. Yale graduate Amy Waldman had an impressive portfolio of clips, including some from *The New York Times*, after two years in South Africa. Although some editors told her she didn't have the requisite newsroom experience, she soon found an editor's job at *Washington Monthly*.

Still, Waldman is vaguely restless. Working in Washington "is nowhere near as exciting as South Africa," she said, and distant lands are beckoning once again. Waldman's sentiments echo those often heard among former freelancers back in the newsroom. "Now I look back," she said, "and wish I hadn't left so soon."

8 BEYOND THE NEWS

S tanding on the wharf at Inhambane, Mozambique, Margaret Knox and Dan Baum watched the rusty cranes load the aging freighter that was to carry them down the coast. Its Danish captain had agreed to take them aboard so that they could bypass the war-ravaged countryside which they had just seen firsthand: the dangerous roads, the hungry beggars, the sullen boy-soldiers toting AK-47s. It was a relief. As the cranes hoisted big bundles of loose cashews aboard the ship, some of the old nets strained, then burst, raining nuts onto the dock and into the harbor. "These golden nuts that somebody had worked so hard to harvest despite the war . . . ," Knox recalled wistfully.

Later that night, as the ship sailed south, the Filipino crew shined flashlights into the inky water and scooped up squid that flocked to the light. The ship's engineer, a Scot with a flair for red sauces, cooked up a feast. Even the gray, pebbly rice tasted great. There was magic in the moment.

"From the beginning, my motivation about becoming a writer was exploring cultures and territories that I hadn't experienced as a child," Knox said. Steaming down the African coast on a rusty freighter, its hold full of cashews and the moist air of the Indian Ocean filling the immense black sky, Knox and Baum knew they had made the right decision in quitting their jobs and coming to Africa. That night, their life was the story.

"I had always wanted to be a foreign correspondent," Knox added, but "really didn't have the instincts for making my way through the politics of a corporation, waiting it out, and playing my cards right to be sent overseas."

She and Baum succeeded as foreign correspondents, and not because they got lucky. Making it as a freelance foreign correspondent has little to do with luck, at least not luck as most people think of it. Although heading abroad as a freelance journalist is a challenge with unpredictable results, it's hardly a wait-and-see venture. In the context of freelancing abroad, good luck is simply the ability to position oneself for sudden opportunities, then recognize and exploit them. In short, luck favors the well prepared. Baum and Knox were primed for success, both professionally and personally.

THE VALUE OF COURAGE, COMMON SENSE, AND HARD WORK

Journalism experience helps a lot, but courage, common sense, and hard work are the main prerequisites for success as a freelance foreign correspondent. It takes courage to head overseas through the mists of uncertainty, leaving behind the safe and the familiar. It takes common sense and hard work to convert that courage into accomplishment. Such accomplishment may come in different forms, and it may come in fits and starts. But keep at it and you will succeed on one level or another.

In October of 1991, nine months after arriving in Spain, John Pollack was making ends meet as a reporter—but just. The money from a recent cover story in *USA Today* was running out, and the expected bonanza of 1992 was still months away. Then the news broke: Israel and the Arab states had agreed to meet in Madrid to talk about peace for the first time. President Bush and President Gorbachev would ceremonially open the talks. Within ten days, an estimated four thousand journalists would converge on the story, transforming Spain into the world's center stage.

Minutes after hearing the announcement, Pollack called *USA Today*'s foreign editor in Washington, offering his services. The next day, he sold a story to his former employer, the *Hartford Courant*. Where previously the paper had relied on him for school board coverage in Plainville, now he was writing about Spanish diplomacy and its relationship to the Middle East peace process.

Inside the official press center, a cavernous convention facility near the eighteenth-century Royal Palace where official negotiations were taking place, Pollack juggled two jobs: one as a production assistant for ABC News, the second as a *USA Today* stringer writing sidebars and doing background reporting for the paper's Big Guns, the staff correspondents sent in from Washington.

One of the *USA Today* reporters introduced Pollack to William Montalbano, the *Los Angeles Times*'s southern Europe correspondent, who had flown in from Rome. "How's your Spanish?" Montalbano asked, gruffly. It didn't seem like a friendly question but more like a challenge.

"*Está bien*," Pollack replied casually, heart pounding.

"Good," Montalbano said evenly. "I may be looking for some help. Send me your stuff." He handed Pollack his business card, and that was the end of the conversation.

After the Middle East Peace Conference had ended, Pollack ($1,500 in his pocket) Xeroxed his clips and résumé and sent them off to Rome. A few weeks later, the phone rang. "This is Bill Montalbano of the *L.A. Times*. I've got an assignment for you . . ."

The working relationship that ensued grew well beyond the

standard back-and-forth between correspondent and fixer. In going to work for Montalbano as the *Los Angeles Times*'s Spain stringer, Pollack acquired both a part-time employer and—more importantly—an exacting mentor.

One of the world's premier foreign correspondents, Montalbano set high standards. He was blunt, demanding, and scant of praise, but he was also extremely generous with his time and expertise. During periodic forays to Spain, he took Pollack along on interviews, assigned him background reporting, and from Italy edited the monthly features Pollack wrote for the paper. That valuable experience, and Montalbano's recommendation, led to a string for the *Miami Herald* and a part-time, local-hire post at The Associated Press.

One day, walking across the broad stones of a Madrid sidewalk, Montalbano asked Pollack, "Why'd you come to Spain?"

"Because I wanted to be a foreign correspondent, and I knew nobody was going to send me," Pollack answered.

"Good for you," Montalbano said.

Was this sequence of events mere good luck? No. From his days in Plainville to his work at the Middle East Peace Conference, Pollack had hustled for every opportunity, embracing and wringing from them everything he possibly could.

INTANGIBLE BENEFITS

Freelancer Ann Marsh found something quite different—a sense of going beyond the news as she bore witness to the history unfolding before her. One wintry day in Bratislava, in 1992, Marsh covered the funeral of Alexander Dubček. Back in 1968, Dubček had led Czechoslovakia through the Prague Spring, until Soviet tanks crushed the peaceful revolution. Hard-line communists had then bundled him off to a long exile in a Slovakian forest; only toward the end of his life did he emerge again as a voice in national politics.

"It was a freezing morning and as snow fell I briefly interviewed then–Czechoslovakian president Vaclav Havel," Marsh said. "At the graveyard I had the surreal experience of standing on the muddy lip of Dubček's grave. Controls were so lax that I feared camera crews would literally tumble down on top of Dubček's plain wooden coffin. I imagined that Dubček would have hated the Soviet-style guards who goose-stepped while his coffin was on view."

Inescapably, freelance foreign correspondents will discover that the benefits of working abroad far exceed mere professional advancement. These realizations may come slowly, perhaps over a steaming cup of espresso in a gilded European café, or while hiking through the Amazon jungle, raucous monkeys taunting you from the leafy canopy above. This sense of being somewhere special usually comes in those moments when the phone stops ringing and, your deadlines met, you start to relax.

It's a chance to reflect on all that you have gained by choosing to live and work outside of your native land. As a freelancer in Spain, Jesse Tinsley studied his flamenco guitar with an ardor approaching that of the Gypsy musicians who inspired him. Was pursuing his passion in Spain worth quitting his secure, unionized staff job at the *Rocky Mountain News*? In a word, yes.

Ultimately, freelancing abroad may not provide the security of a 9-to-5, but it offers something that to many people is equally enticing: independence.

"There is more freedom as a freelancer," Alan Riding said, reflecting on his years as a stringer in Mexico. "I sometimes yearn for that freedom."

Poet Walt Whitman best captures the essence of this freedom in his "Song of the Open Road," excerpted below.

> Afoot and light-hearted I take to the open road,
> Healthy, free, the world before me,
> The long brown path before me leading wherever I choose.

Henceforth I ask not good fortune, I myself am good
    fortune,
Henceforth I whimper no more, postpone no more, need
    nothing,
Done with indoor complaints, libraries, querulous
    criticisms,
Strong and content I travel the open road.

The earth, that is sufficient,
I do not want the constellations any nearer,
I know they are very well where they are,
I know they suffice for those who belong to them. . . .

. . . From this hour I ordain myself loos'd of limits and
    imaginary lines,
Going where I list, my own master total and absolute,
Listening to others, considering well what they say,
Pausing, searching, receiving, contemplating,
Gently, but with undeniable will, divesting myself of the
    holds that would hold me.

Whitman wrote more than poetry. He also worked as a free-lance journalist. In both endeavors, he used words to explore. Reporting from abroad is all about exploration—not just of specific foreign lands and cultures but of your own self, the way you think and the way you see the world. With careful planning, hard work, persistence, and talent, you too can make your own road as a freelance foreign correspondent.

APPENDIX 1

Is Freelancing Abroad Right for You?

Most successful escapes are predicated on solid preparation, and the purpose of this worksheet is to help you think through the pros and cons of moving abroad as a freelance foreign correspondent.

Consider the following list of questions, which are by no means exhaustive. Rather, the questions provide a framework for thought. Although you've no doubt already tackled some of these questions at various points in your life, your ability to clearly articulate honest answers now will be essential to making a good decision about whether to try freelancing overseas. The authors suggest you answer them on paper, then discuss your responses with a trusted friend or colleague.

1. What are your professional goals?
What are you doing to reach these goals?
How do your current job and other principal activities relate to these goals?
What could you be doing to get more out of your current situation?
When do you expect to achieve your goals?
What are your current professional obligations?
Are you satisfied with your job?
Are you having fun?

2. *What are your personal goals?*
What are you doing to reach these goals?
How does your current social situation relate to your personal goals?
What could you be doing to get more out of your current situation?
When do you expect to achieve these goals?
Are you satisfied with your social life most of the time?

3. *What are your family obligations?*
How and when might these change?

4. *If you could do anything with your life right now, you would . . .*

5. *Why are you thinking about becoming a foreign correspondent?*
What would be the best and worst aspects of such a move, professionally and personally?
Are you interested in foreign cultures? Why or why not?
How might a move abroad relate to your professional growth?
How might a move abroad relate to your personal growth?
Do you think you'd like to immerse yourself in another culture and language?

6. *What is your financial situation?*
Current income?
Living expenses?
Outstanding debts?
Long-term financial goals?

7. *What is the opportunity cost, if any, of going abroad?*
Lost income?
Lost job opportunities?
Lost social opportunities?

8. *What is the opportunity cost, if any, of staying in your current situation?*
Boredom?
Frustration?
Professional stagnation?
Wasted years?

APPENDIX 2

Sources and Contacts

Publications

Benn's Medial (volumes I-III)
Editor & Publisher International Yearbook
Gale's Directory of Publications and Broadcast Media
Gale's Encyclopedia of Associations and Association Periodicals
Gale's Newsletters in Print
National Register Publishing's Magazines & International Publications
National Register Publishing's Newspaper Directory
National Register Publishing's TV & Radio Yearbook
R. R. Bowker's Broadcasting & Cable Yearbook
Willings' Press Guide (volumes I–II)

Embassies and Consulates

For aspiring foreign correspondents in North America who are planning to go abroad as freelancers, information about embassies and consulates representing some principal English-speaking countries is available from the sources listed below. For stringers currently located elsewhere, a good place to seek similar information is through the desired embassy in the nearest capital (i.e., the U.S. embassy in London).

United States of America
Publication: "U.S. Department of State: Key Officers of Foreign Service Posts"
Superintendent of Documents
U.S. Government Printing Office
Washington, DC 20402
Phone: (202) 512-1800
Fax: (202) 512-2168

Canada
Publication: "Canadian Representatives Abroad"
Canada Communications Group
Ottawa, Canada K1A OS9
Phone: (819) 956-4800
Fax: (819) 956-7620

Great Britain
Embassy of the Kingdom of Great Britain and Northern Ireland
3100 Massachusetts Ave., N.W.
Washington, DC 20008

Phone: (202) 462-1340
In the United Kingdom, dial "153" to British Telecom's International Directory Inquiries.

Australia
Embassy of Australia
1601 Massachusetts Ave., N.W.
Washington, DC 20036
Phone: (202) 797-3000

South Africa
Embassy of South Africa
3051 Massachusetts Ave., N.W.
Washington, DC 20008
Phone: (202) 232-4400

New Zealand
Embassy of New Zealand
37 Observatory Circle N.W.
Washington, DC 20008
Phone: (202) 328-4800

Other Useful Contacts

The Committee to Protect Journalists maintains up-to-date information on issues and events affecting the safety of journalists worldwide. The National Writers Union and American Citizens Abroad serve U.S. citizens primarily. Similar organizations exist for citizens of the United Kingdom and other English-speaking nations.

National Writers Union
873 Broadway, #203
New York, NY 10003
U.S.A.
Phone: (212) 254-0279
Fax: (212) 254-0673
E-mail: nwu@netcom.com
Web site:
  http://www.nwu.org/nwu

Committee to Protect Journalists
330 Seventh Avenue, 12th Floor
New York, NY 10001
U.S.A.
Phone: (212) 465-1004
Fax: (212) 465-9568
E-mail: info@cpj.org
Web site: http://www.cpj.org

American Citizens Abroad
P.O. Box 321
CH-1211 Geneva 12
Switzerland
Phone and fax: (41-22) 347-6847
E-mail: acage@aca.ch
Web site: http://www.aca.ch

Equipment Checklist

The equipment listed below will enable you to operate abroad as a foreign correspondent with efficiency and effectiveness. Before buying any electrical appliances, be sure to ascertain the voltage, current, and electrical plug type in your target country, and make sure that your equipment is compatible or that you have the required adapters. If necessary, consult the equipment manufacturer for details. Note that the list does not include gear for those intending to freelance for TV; such equipment is prohibitively expensive and best rented at the outset.

- Laptop computer with an internal fax/modem
- Software (word-processing, communications, and a Web browser)
- Portable printer, with extra ink cartridges
- Camera, flash, and film
- Portable tape recorder
- Phone/answering machine
- Long phone cord with two male ends
- Alligator clips and electrical tape
- Small screwdriver set
- Short-wave radio with earplug or headphones
- Hi-8 camera (optional)

APPENDIX 3
Sample Phone Log

Phone companies in some countries do not itemize your phone bill. In other countries, calls are itemized but the bills arrive months after the calls were made. For timely reimbursement from your media for calls made while working on their stories, careful record-keeping is essential.

Always send the actual itemized phone bill from the telephone company, if available. If not, contact the phone company to ascertain phone rates, and keep your own master log of phone calls. Separate calls into categories: local, long-distance, international calling card, and mobile phone. It's a hassle, but will eventually save you time and money because media rarely pay for nonitemized phone bills. When submitting for reimbursement from your clients, include a copy of the phone company's description of its charges according to time of day, duration of call, and distance involved.

The following is a sample of Al Goodman's phone log for a *New York Times* job:

Al Goodman phone calls from Madrid via Spanish Telefónica and AT&T for *New York Times* Travel Section Question/Answer on "Studying Catalan" in Barcelona

TELEFÓNICA LONG DISTANCE CALLS

Date	To/Purpose	Time	Minutes	Pesetas
June 17	Barcelona/Generalitat	11:25 am	1	79
June 17	Barcelona/lang. school	11:30 am	4	243
June 18	Barcelona/lang. school	12:20 pm	1	79
June 18	Barcelona/lang. school	1:05 pm	8	432
June 19	Barcelona/Amer. Consulate	12:07 pm	5	295
June 19	Gironella/lang. festival	12:12 pm	3	184

Long Distance Calls (Pesetas)	1,312
Telefónica Total (Pesetas)	1,312
Telefónica Dollar Equivalent	$10.50

AT&T Calls

June 19	NYT/MacNeille	6:30 pm	11	$12.54

Telephone Total (Telefonica & AT&T)	$23.04

APPENDIX 4
Sample Invoice

Good record-keeping is part of any successful small business; free-lancing abroad is no different. Many media won't pay freelancers until they receive an invoice, so send one promptly if you seek timely payment. Here's a sample invoice that Al Goodman might send to CNN, with jargon explained in parentheses for the reader's benefit. He numbers the invoices sequentially, by year, with invoice 1 to media A; invoice 2 to media B; invoice 3 to media A; and so forth.

Invoice No. 020-1996 from Al Goodman, CNN-Madrid

To: John Smith
CNN International Desk
1 CNN Center
Box 105366
Atlanta, GA 30348
U.S.A.

Invoice Date: May 7, 1996
Work Dates: Various dates in April–May 1996
Work Type: Reporting/live beeper *(phone interview with the anchorman)*/voice tracks *(recorded voice)* over video images
Work Location: Madrid, Spain
Purpose: Beepers and voice tracks for new Aznar government

Amount Due: U.S. $558.05

Sum of:
1. $ 50.00   April 25 beeper with anchorman J. Mann. Court
             clears González in dirty war.
2. $ 50.00   April 26 beeper w/J. Mann: Aznar tries to get support
             of Catalans for government.
3. $ 50.00   May 3 voice-track: Aznar investiture debate begins.
4. $100.00   May 4 beeper w/Denise Dillon and voice tracks: Aznar
             wins investiture debate in Parliament.
5. $100.00   May 5 beeper w/Veronica Pedrosa and voice tracks:
             Aznar is sworn in as new prime minister.
6. $100.00   May 6 beeper w/J. Mann and voice tracks: Aznar's
             new government ministers get started on job.
7. $108.05   Recent phone calls for CNN. See enclosed phone list.

Please *transfer* the payment directly to my bank account:
    Alan Goodman
    Account number: 123-456-789-1
    Routing number: 123-456-789
    Name of bank: AnyBank, Inc.
    Bank's address: 123 Main Street
                       St. Louis, MO 123245
    Bank's phone: (314) 123-4567

(Goodman's Social Security number: 123-45-6789)

Thank you very much.

Alan Goodman   Madrid telephone: (34-1) 123-4567

APPENDIX 5

Foreign Electricity Guide

Listed on the next two pages are popularly traveled countries, their electrical information, and the appropriate adaptor plugs for each.

A   B   C   D   E

Country	Plug	Outlet	Volts	Freq./Hz.	Country	Plug	Outlet	Volts	Freq./Hz.
Afghanistan	E	10	220	50	Ethiopia	B, E	2, 5, 10	220	50
Albania	B	2	220	50	Fiji	C	8	240	50
Algeria	B, E	2, 10	127/220	50	Finland	B	2	230	50
American Samoa	A, B, C	1, 2, 8	120/220	60	France	B	3	230	50
Angola	B	2	220	50	Georgia	B	2	220	50
Anguilla	D	9	240	50	Germany	B	2	230	50
Antigua	A, D	1, 9	230	60	Ghana	B, D, E	2, 9, 10	220	50
Argentina	B, C	2, 8	220	50	Greece	B	2	230	50
Armenia	B	2	220	50	Greenland	B	4	220	50
Aruba	A, B	1, 2	115	60	Grenada	B, D, E	2, 9, 10	230	50
Australia	C	8	240	50	Guadeloupe	B	2, 3	220	50
Austria	B	2	230	50	Guam	A	1	120	60
Azerbaijan	B	2	220	50	Guatemala	A	1	120	60
Azores	B, E	2, 10	220	50	Guinea	B	2	220	50
Bahamas	A	1	120	60	Guyana	A	1	110	60
Bahrain	D, E	9, 10	220	50	Haiti	A	1	110	60
Bangladesh	B, E	2, 10	220	50	Honduras	A	1	110	60
Barbados	A	1	115	50	Hong Kong	D	9	220	50
Belarus	B	2	220	50	Hungary	B	2	220	50
Belgium	B	2	230	50	Iceland	B	2	220	50
Belize	A	1	110	60	India	B, E	2, 10	220	50
Benin	E	10	220	50	Indonesia	B	2	220	50
Bermuda	A	1	120	60	Iran	B	2	220	50
Bolivia	A, B	1, 2	110/220	50	Iraq	B, D, E	2, 9, 10	220	50
Bosnia-Herzegovina	B	2	220	50	Ireland	D	9	220	50
Botswana	D, E	9, 10	220	50	Israel	B	7	230	50
Brazil	A, B	1, 2	110/220	60	Italy	B	5	230	50
Bulgaria	B	2	220	50	Ivory Coast	B	2	220	50
Burkina	B	2	220	50	Jamaica	A	1	110	50
Burma	D, E	9, 10	230	50	Japan	A	1	100	50/60
Burundi	B	2	220	50	Jordan	B, D	2, 9	220	50
Cambodia	A, B	1, 2	120/220	50	Kazakhstan	B	2	220	50
Cameroon	B	2	220	50	Kenya	B, E	2, 10	240	50
Canada	A	1	120	60	Kirghizia	B	2	220	50
Canary Islands	B	2, 3	220	50	Korea	A, B	1, 2	110/220	50/60
Cayman Islands	A	1	120	60	Kuwait	B, D, E	2, 9, 10	240	50
Central African Rep.	B	2	220	50	Laos	A, B	1, 2	220	50
Chad	B, E	2, 10	220	50	Latvia	B	2	220	50
Chile	B	2, 5	220	50	Lebanon	B	2	220	50
China	B, C	2, 8	220	50	Lesotho	B, E	2, 10	240	50
Colombia	A	1	110	60	Liberia	A, D	1, 9	120	60
Comoros	B	3	220	50	Libya	B, E	5, 10	230	50
Congo	B	2	220	50	Liechtenstein	B	6	220	50
Costa Rica	A	1	120	60	Lithuania	B	2	220	50
Croatia	B	2	220	50	Luxembourg	B	2	230	50
Cuba	A	1	120	60	Macao	B, E	2, 10	220	50
Curacao	A, B	1, 2	110/220	60	Macedonia	B	2	220	50
Cyprus	B, D	2, 9	240	50	Madagascar	B	2, 3	220	50
Czech Republic	B	2	220	50	Malawi	D	9	230	50
Denmark	B	4	230	50	Malaysia	D	9	240	50
Djibouti	B	2, 3	220	50	Mali	B	2, 3	220	50
Dominica	B, D	2, 9	230	50	Malta	D	9	240	50
Dominican Rep.	A	1	110	60	Martinique	B	2, 3	220	50
Ecuador	A	1	120	60	Mauritania	B	2	220	50
Egypt	B	2	220	50	Mauritius	B, D, E	2, 9, 10	230	50
El Salvador	A	1	115	60	Mexico	A	1	120	60
Eritrea	B, E	2, 10	220	50	Moldova	B	2	220	50
Estonia	B	2	220	50	Monaco	B	2, 3	220	50
England	D	9	240	50	Mongolia	B	2	220	50

Country	Plug	Outlet	Volts	Freq./Hz.
Morocco	B, E	2, 10	220	50
Mozambique	B	2	220	50
Namibia	E	10	220	50
Nepal	E	10	220	50
Netherlands	B	2	230	50
New Zealand	C	8	230	50
Nicaragua	A	1	120	60
Niger	B	2	220	50
Nigeria	D, E	9, 10	230	50
Norway	B	2	230	50
Oman	D, E	9, 10	240	50
Pakistan	B, E	2, 10	230	50
Panama	A	1	120	60
Papua New Guinea	C	8	240	50
Paraguay	B	2	220	50
Peru	A, B	1, 2	110/220	50/60
Philippines	A, B	1, 2	110/220	60
Poland	B	2	220	50
Portugal	B, E	2, 10	230	50
Puerto Rico	A	1	120	60
Qatar	D, E	9, 10	240	50
Romania	B	2	220	50
Russian Federation	B	2	220	50
Rwanda	B	2	220	50
St. Kitts-Nevis	D, E	9, 10	230	60
St. Lucia	D	9	240	50
St. Vincent	D	9	230	50
Saudi Arabia	A, B, D	1, 3, 9	127/220	50/60
Senegal	B	2	220	50
Seychelles	D, E	9, 10	240	50
Scotland	D	9	220	50
Sierra Leone	D, E	9, 10	230	50
Singapore	B, D, E	2, 9, 10	230	50
Slovakia	B	2	220	50
Slovenia	B	2	220	50
Somalia	B	2	220	50
South Africa	E	10	230	50
Spain	B	2	230	50
Sri Lanka	E	10	230	50
Sudan	B, D	2, 9	240	50
Surinam	A,B	1	110/220	50/60
Swaziland	E	10	230	50
Sweden	B	2	230	50
Switzerland	B	6	230	50
Syria	B	2	220	50
Tahiti	A, B	1,3	127/220	50/60
Taiwan	A	1	110	60
Tajikistan	B	2	220	50
Tanzania	D, E	9, 10	230	50
Thailand	A, B	1, 2	220	50
Tonga	A, C	1, 8	110/220	50/60
Trinidad & Tobago	A, D	1, 9	115/230	60
Tunisia	B	2, 5	220	50
Turkey	B	2	220	50
Turkmenistan	B	2	220	50
Uganda	D, E	9, 10	240	50
Ukraine	B	2	220	50
United Arab Emirates	D, E	9, 10	220	50
United States	A	1	120	60
Uruguay	B	2	220	50
Uzebekistan	B	2	220	50
Venezuela	A	1	120	60
Vietnam	A, B	1, 3	120/220	50
Virgin Islands	A	1	120	60
Wales	D	9	220	50
Western Samoa	C	8	230	50
Yemen	B, D, E	2, 9, 10	220	50
Yugoslavia	B	2	220	50
Zaire	B, E	2, 10	220	50
Zambia	B, D	2, 9	220	50
Zimbabwe	D, E	9, 10	220	50

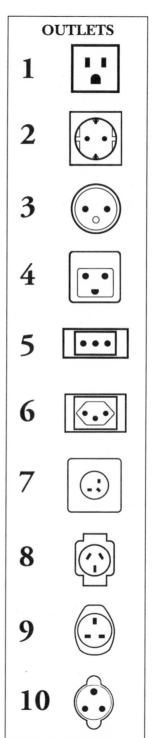

OUTLETS

1
2
3
4
5
6
7
8
9
10

INDEX

About This Book

Freelancers John Pollack and Al Goodman were drinking dry sherry in a crowded Madrid bar late one night after their staff colleagues from major media—in town to cover the opening of an important art museum—had turned in at their hotels. "You should write a book about all of your experiences here," Pollack told Goodman. "No, that's crazy," Goodman said, laughing. Looking about the room of raucous, happy Spaniards and stacked barrels of sherry, Pollack got a sudden burst of inspiration. "I know," Pollack said. "We'll write it together. 'How to Become a Freelance Foreign Correspondent'!"

That was in 1992, and the pair got right to work, raising their glasses in a toast and outlining the project on a paper napkin. One agent, two book proposals, two years, and many rejection letters later, Pollack's enthusiasm was unabated. Though wary of investing more time and effort, Goodman conceded that the project was too good to die. Stubborn freelancers, they forged ahead to write the book anyway, on speculation.

But by this time Pollack had returned to the United States, and e-mail was the only feasible way to handle a trans-Atlantic book project without going broke on the telephone. So, for nearly a year and almost entirely over the Internet, Goodman and Pollack hammered out a manuscript that Henry Holt and Company—alone among dozens of publishers—recognized had potential. But it still needed work. So Goodman and Pollack went back to their laptops, meeting only o⬛ their modems do most of the talking. ⬛ conceived in a sherry bar and born⬛ uct of their collaboration.

About the Authors

AL GOODMAN is a Spain-based stringer for *The New York Times*, CNN, National Public Radio, and the *Wine Spectator*.

JOHN POLLACK, who now lives in Washington, D.C., was a stringer in Spain for the *Los Angeles Times*, the *Miami Herald*, *USA Today*, and The Associated Press.

WOLF BLITZER is CNN's Senior White House Correspondent. He began his career in journalism as a stringer for the Reuters News Agency in its Tel Aviv bureau in 1972.